Colonel Arthur
("

C000016597

Fifty Breakfasts

A splendid Victorian collection of over
130 classic breakfast recipes

JEPPESTOWN

Also available from Jeppestown Press

Where the Lion Roars: An 1890 African Colonial Cookery Book

The Bulawayo Cookery Book and Household Guide

The Anglo-African Who's Who 1907

Matabeleland and the Victoria Falls

With Captain Stairs to Katanga

The Ghana Cookery Book

Cooking in West Africa

The Imperial African Cookery Book

Five-O'-Clock Tea

www.jeppestown.com

Colonel Arthur R. Kenney-Herbert
(*"Wyvern"*)

Fifty Breakfasts

JEPPESTOWN

Introduction

Colonel Arthur Kenney-Herbert (1840-1916) is best known for his masterful book *Culinary Jottings for Madras*, published in 1878 while he was an officer in the Madras Cavalry, and based on a series of scholarly cooking articles written for the *Madras Athenaeum and Daily News*.

Following his retirement in 1892 he returned to London and founded the School of the Common-Sense Cookery Association, teaching the art of cooking and giving celebrated public lectures and cookery demonstrations on topics ranging from curry to vegetarianism.

As one might expect, an Indian influence is evident throughout his breakfast recipes—Mushroom Curry and Rice, for example, or his simple but utterly authentic recipe for Appams (*"Apums"*), the little pancakes made from coconut milk and rice flour that are such a feature of South Indian breakfasts. But you will find that his recipes cover every possible glorious permutation of every imaginable breakfast delicacy— from Fried Eggs and Bacon, Calves' Liver and Crumpets to Grilled Partridge.

While some of his other books have been republished in the recent past, Jeppestown Press is delighted to offer the first reprint of Colonel Kenney-Herbert's *Fifty Breakfasts* for almost a century.

FIFTY BREAKFASTS

BY

A. KENNEY HERBERT

("*Wyvern*")

"CORDON ROUGE," AUTHOR OF "COMMONSENSE COOKERY," ETC.

FIFTH IMPRESSION

London

EDWARD ARNOLD

1908

CONTENTS.

———◆◇◆———

INTRODUCTION.

THESE little breakfast *menus* are designed for a family or party of six : each will be found to contain a dish of fish, a meat dish, and a dish of eggs, any two of which can be selected if three be considered too many. Seven of them are composed for days of abstinence. A plate of fancy bread is suggested for every *menu* to facilitate choice, recipes for which will be found in the Appendix.

The dishes that have been described will be found practicable by a large section of the community ; for while many of the recipes as they stand may be suited to those with whom a very careful consideration of kitchen economy is unnecessary, by the exercise of a little discretion expensive adjuncts such as chopped ham, tongue, mushrooms, &c., can of course be very easily omitted without sacrificing much of the general tastiness of the dishes themselves, and thus bring them within the reach of all readers of the treatise.

It will be seen that I have propounded to a great extent tasty *réchauffés* of fish and meat rather than dishes requiring fresh ingredients. At first sight some of these may be considered troublesome, but I would here point out that, in order to provide nice little dishes for breakfast, it is absolutely necessary that the cook should effect some portion of their preparation on the evening of the previous day. She rarely has sufficient time in the morning for much delicate work of course, yet with a little forethought this can be combated, and the whole category of *croquettes*, *rissoles*, *petits caises*, &c., be brought into play without difficulty. If the meat or fish required for such dishes be prepared and set in the sauce overnight the process the next morning is both simple and expeditious. In the same way hashes, stews, *ragoûts*, &c., can be re-heated in the *bain-marie*, and will be found all the better for having marinaded all night in their well-flavoured sauces. The "stitch in time" accomplished during the afternoon, or before the kitchen fire is let down at night, "saves nine" at the busy hour before breakfast the next day. Indeed the ding-dong monotony of " bacon and eggs " alternated with " eggs and bacon " of many English breakfast tables is wholly inexcusable, so easy is it to provide variety with the exercise of a little consideration.

For the " warming-up " process there is nothing so safe as the *bain-marie*. This is a utensil which it is to be hoped every one possesses. Stews, curries, hashes, &c., can thus be re-heated without deterioration, or fear of burning, boiling, or other mishap.

As another most capital thing for the preparation of breakfast dishes, I strongly advocate the use of the Dutch oven. This is an old-fashioned contrivance, no doubt, but cheap, and especially handy for the fast cooking of fish and heating *gratins*. It can be placed in front of the fire closely or at a slight distance according to the degree of heat required, and the cook can see how things placed within it are getting on. This alone gives it an advantage over the ordinary oven, while the food half-baked half-roasted by its means seems crisper and more appetising.

Baking dishes in sizes, *caisses*, and scallop shells of white fire-proof, Limoges ware are to be recommended for use in connection with break-fast. They can be set without risk in the Dutch or common oven, and afford a method of serving minces, re-cooked fish, eggs, and " remains," at once tasteful and inviting.

Fried fish is, as a rule, a popular thing for breakfast, and if the cook bear in mind that *second* frying by no means spoils fillets, &c., that may have been so cooked the evening before, she will readily fall back on this method of re-cooking them. A plunge of two or three minutes' duration into very hot fat is all that is required, followed by draining, drying carefully, and service on a hot napkin. Soles should be cross-cut in pieces two and a half inches wide, or filleted, and whitings are much nicer when not curled round in the manner so invariably adopted by London fishmongers.

A propos of frying, I take it for granted that in all well-regulated kitchens a supply of good, stale, oven-dried, and finely sifted white crumbs, as well as a bottle of well-rasped light-brown crust, is always kept ready for use. Fresh spongy crumbs are wholly unfit for " breading " cutlets, *croquettes*, fish, and so on. Finely grated, hard, dry, mild cheese—not necessarily Parmesan or Gruyère—should always be similarly stored.

An almost essentially necessary article in this branch of cookery is a *wire drainer*—such as confectioners use. Upon this *croquettes, rissoles,* fried fillets, even a fried sole, can be set to dry thoroughly after draining, for which purpose the drainer should either be placed in the mouth of the oven—the door ajar—or in front of the fire.

For little *fritures* such as whitebait a wire frying basket is of course indispensable.

In composing the recipes given in this little series I have done my best to avoid perplexing generalities : "some" of this, "a little" of that, and so on. The quantity of each thing, either by weight or measure of capacity, has been put down as accurately as possible. Still it often happens that very small allotments such as the exact proportions of a seasoning must be given in conventional terms, as, for instance, "a pinch" of pepper. This quantity, to be very particular, might be counted as one-eighth of an ounce. Then a breakfast cup should hold half a pint, an afternoon tea-cup one gill and a half, a coffee-cup one gill.

I frequently mention "spiced pepper." This is a kind of herbaceous mixture which I strongly advise every cook to make for herself in the autumn each year when the herbs are finally gathered. It comes in most handily for seasonings in pies, forcemeats, stuffings, and in the flavouring of nearly every *réchauffé.* Mine, adapted from that of Gouffé, is made as follows :

DOMESTIC SPICED PEPPER.

One ounce of mixed thyme, marjoram, rosemary, and bay-leaf, carefully picked and thoroughly dried, pounded, and sifted, the mixture being allotted in these proportions, two thirds thyme and bay-leaf to one third marjoram and rosemary. Half an ounce of powdered mace, the same of nutmeg, a quarter of an ounce of finely ground black pepper, and one-eighth of an ounce of Nepaul pepper. Mix after carefully sifting each ingredient, and put the mixture into a well-dried bottle. This can obviously be doubled or increased to any extent.

One ounce of the above with four ounces of salt gives a useful " spiced salt."

A little wine is occasionally recommended in flavouring sauces, &c. ; for this I have chosen Marsala, which, if of a reliable quality, is the best that can be used for domestic cookery, and, if the truth be told, the equivalent of Madeira at many a pretentious restaurant.

Cream is a very excellent thing—so excellent, indeed, that in the cookery of the present day its use is far too indiscriminate. In breakfast dishes it is to my mind quite out of place, while in the course of a dinner the less often it is introduced the better. Those who like it can of course direct their cooks accordingly.

The most wholesome and handy way of boiling eggs for the breakfast table may be thus described :—

Put a small saucepan over a methylated spirit lamp, which can be placed on a side table. When the water boils put in the eggs, and in ten seconds put out the lamp, covering the saucepan closely. In eight minutes an ordinary hen's egg will be ready, the albumen soft, and the yolk nicely formed. The common method of boiling eggs at a gallop for three minutes has the effect of over-cooking the albumen and rendering it indigestible, while the yolk is scarcely done at all.

Good tea and coffee are, it need scarcely be said, important elements of a good English breakfast. To secure them it is really necessary, after having chosen the tea and coffee that suit you best, to be liberal in dispensing them. A proper cup of either is out of the question if the allowance be too narrowly curtailed. The practice of doling out tea by carefully measured teaspoonfuls (handed down to us by our elderly maiden aunts) was perhaps necessary in the days when the only leaf in the market came from China and cost from four to five shillings a pound. The required strength was then obtained by the pernicious system of setting the tea " to draw." People now, however, have come to understand that to be wholesome tea must be produced by rapid infusion, not by a long process of steeping, and in order to get this at its best a good allowance of the leaf is necessary. Teapots are to be got with perforated cylinders to hold the tea, which can be withdrawn after an infusion of five minutes.

In this way a capital and quite harmless cup of tea can easily be produced.

For coffee-making there are numerous inventions more or less ingenious, but after all for really satisfactory, easy, and rapid action nothing surpasses the percolator—"Hutchinson's patent" for choice. A tablespoonful of coffee powder per breakfastcupful of coffee is a fair allowance.

Lastly, I would advise all who like things *hot* at breakfast to invest in one of Messrs. Wolff and Co's "universal heaters," sold at 119, New Bond Street, an excellent contrivance for keeping dishes, milk, coffee, &c., hot in the breakfast-room without deterioration, superseding the somewhat cumbersome practice of placing dishes before the fire, and of course a boon during the months when fires are dispensed with.

WYVERN.

LONDON, *Feb.* 5, 1894.

MENU I.

Baked fish in scallop shells.

Kidneys à la brochette.

Buttered eggs with vegetablcs.

Muffins.

THIS is to be composed of any cold fish and sauce left the previous evening. Pick the fish from the bones; measure the quantity *1. Baked* (a pound will be enough for six nice *fish in* scallops), add one third of its bulk of *scallop* white crumbs; season with a salt- *shells.* spoonful of spiced pepper and one of salt; let this rest awhile. Put the bones, skin, and especially the head, into a small saucepan, with an onion sliced, a teaspoonful of salt, and six black peppercorns; cover this with milk and water (half-and-half), and stir into it a teaspoonful of anchovy sauce; set to boil, then simmer fifteen minutes; strain; thicken slightly, using half an

ounce of butter and half an ounce of flour to a
full breakfastcup of the broth ; mix smoothly,
stirring in any sauce that may have been left the
previous evening.   Now butter six scallop shells,
or one medium-sized fire-proof baking dish ;
arrange the picked fish and crumbs therein,
scattering a layer of finely minced parsley over
it ; moisten thoroughly with the sauce, strew a
layer of crust raspings over the surface, heat up
in the Dutch oven, and send up on a folded
napkin.

N.B.—If the fish was boiled the previous
evening, use the gelatinous water in which it
was cooked instead of milk and water in pre-
paring the sauce.   Fish-boilings should never be
thrown away.

The kidneys in this instance are broiled on
skewers (*brochettes*—*i.e.*, little spits), which are *not*
to be removed.   Take six kidneys ; cut
2. *Kidneys*   six thin slices of bacon two inches long
à la bro-
chette.   and an inch and a half wide ; select
three skewers (plated or wooden) about
seven inches long ; mince a tablespoonful of
parsley as finely as possible ; place an ounce of
butter ready.   See that the gridiron is clean ;
warm, and oil it.   Now cut open each kidney
in the usual manner without quite dividing the
halves, peel off the skin, and pass the skewers
through them, two kidneys on each skewer, with

a piece of bacon, threaded by the skewer, over each kidney. Broil over a brisk fire, cooking the *cut* side of the kidneys first three minutes, then the other side for three minutes. When done put the impaled kidneys and bacon on a hot silver dish ; melt the butter, stir in the minced parsley, add the juice of half a lemon, and pour this over them. Serve as hot as possible.

Vegetables, such as greens, spinach, flower of cauliflowers, beans, peas, &c., that may have been left the previous evening come in most usefully for breakfast. This 3. *Buttered* is too often overlooked. One nice way *eggs with vegetables.* of serving them is on toast with a surface dressing of buttered eggs. Melt half an ounce of butter, or put a coffeecupful of broth or milk into a saucepan, stir into it the vegetables, which, if greens, French beans, or cauliflowers, should be cut up rather small. Season with pepper, salt, and a dust of nutmeg, put into the *bain-marie*, and when steaming hot turn them out neatly over six neat squares of fried bread laid upon a hot dish, spreading the buttered eggs over them. A dusting of finely grated cheese over the surface is an improvement.

Buttered eggs for six people :—Required six eggs, three ounces of butter, a small coffeecupful of milk or good white sauce, a small salt-spoonful of salt and the same of white pepper. Melt half the butter in a roomy stewpan ; break the eggs, mix, season, and stir them into the butter over a low fire ; whisk well with a whisk until *beginning* to set, then add the other half of the butter and, changing the whisk for a wooden spoon, continue stirring for two minutes longer, add the milk or sauce, when the consistency will be correct. The addition of the second half of the butter should be effected by degrees, to facilitate which it should be cut into small pieces beforehand. The stirring must on no account be relaxed during the cookery of buttered eggs, and the dish should not be kept waiting when ready. A spoonful of *Béchamel* sauce, if available, may be used instead of the milk, or ordinary white sauce.

MENU II.

Fresh herrings au gratin.

Hashed mutton with fried bacon.

Omelette with herbs.

Scones.

BUTTER a flat *gratin* dish, sprinkle a layer of chopped parsley over its surface ; lay four nice fresh herrings (trimmed and cleaned) upon this, season well with pepper and 4. *Fresh herrings au gratin.* salt, shake a canopy of raspings and pour a few drops of melted butter over the upper sides of the herrings ; put the dish thus prepared into the Dutch-oven, place this at a moderate distance from the fire, and watch the fish narrowly for a minute or two ; baste with a little more melted butter, push nearer to the fire for the last minute, and serve the dish, as it is, on a folded napkin.

For mustard sauce (if liked) :—melt an ounce of butter in a saucepan ; stir into it an ounce of flour ; when thoroughly mixed add slowly, off the fire, a dessertspoonful of French mustard, incorporating it with the *roux* thoroughly ; next add half a pint of water or broth, let it come to the boil, and pass through the pointed strainer into a hot sauce boat.

The hash ought to be prepared—partly—overnight, viz. :—cut up as much cold mutton in slices as will suffice for the party ; trim 5. *Hashed* off all skin and superfluous fat, dredge *mutton with fried* a layer of flour over the slices, and *bacon.* leave them for the present ; next prepare the best sauce you can for your hash by boiling together the bones and trimmings of the mutton, an onion, a piece of celery, half a carrot, and a teaspoonful of dried sweet herbs, with half an ounce of glaze, or a teaspoonful of bovril, and sufficient water to cover all ingredients. When the best broth possible has been thus obtained, strain, thicken, and flavour it with one teaspoonful of red-currant jelly melted, a tablespoonful of vinegar from the walnut pickle, half a sherry-glass of Harvey sauce, half one of mushroom ketchup, and half one of *Marsala*. Put the sliced mutton into the sauce in a china vegetable dish, cover it from the dust, and set it in a cold larder till morning, when it will only require gentle heating up over a low fire, or in the *bain-marie*. It must on no account boil. Serve in a hot *entrée* dish with

curls of crisply fried bacon and fried bread
sippets as garnish.

I follow two methods of making an *omelette*.
One I explain now, the other later on. This
recipe is for an *omelette* " by the first
intention "—a rapidly made and very   6. *Omelette*
digestible one. For six persons I re- *with herbs.*
commend two small, rather than one large one,
as being more manageable—especially at first.
Nothing is more likely to produce a failure than
an over-full pan. Break three eggs into one
bowl, and three into another, put a saltspoonful
of salt to each, with a dessertspoonful of chopped
parsley, a teaspoonful of finely minced chives or
shallot, one of chervil, and a pinch of pepper. Do
not add milk, or cream, or water. Stir the eggs, and
seasoning well together, and beat only sufficiently
to effect mixture. Choose a roomy *omelette* pan
not less than ten inches in diameter ; see that it
is dry and perfectly clean. Set it over a fast,
clear fire, and put a lump of butter into it the
size of a small hen's egg. Let this melt, and
throw off all water ; as soon as bubbling ceases
the pan is hot enough ; pour the contents of one
of the bowls over its surface. At the moment
of contact the part of the mixture nearest to the
pan will set, gently lift this with a spoon, tip the
pan over a little and let the unformed liquid run
under it ; this will also form ; now give a few good

shakes, and with your spoon coax the *omelette* to slide out of the *omelette* pan into the hot *entrée* dish ready for it. If carefully done the *omelette* will roll over, enveloping within it the partly formed mixture that remained on its surface, and on reaching the dish will spread itself rather, retaining no specially oval or bolsterlike shape, with a little of the juicy golden mixture escaping from its edges. *Omelettes* that are presented in neat crescent or elongated oval shapes are as a rule *puddings* in their consistency, over-cooked, and heavy.

After turning out the first *omelette*, wipe the pan, do not wash it, and repeat the same process with the second basin of mixture, sending the *omelettes* to table "hot and hot," so to speak. A small pat of butter, and chopped parsley should be put into the dish before the *omelette* is turned into it. Timed by the seconds-hand of a watch this *omelette* takes forty-five seconds from the moment of being poured into the pan to that of its being turned into the dish. Be sure that the pan is hot enough to receive the mixture in the first instance, and that the fire is brisk beneath it while frying ; a powerful gas boiling-stove, circular in shape like the "Regina," is suitable for this work.

N.B.—If the chives and chervil were omitted this would be an *omelette au persil* An *omelette aux fines herbes* is made with a totally different garniture.

MENU III.

Fried whitings; maître d'hôtel butter.

Devilled fowl; chutney sauce (Indian).

Ham toast, with poached eggs.

Hot rolls.

————

BREAD-CRUMB and fry the whitings—four nice ones enough—using plenty of very hot fat, in a deep pan ; dish them on a neat fish- *7. Fried* paper, accompanied by plainly melted *whitings ;* *maître d'hôtel* butter served in a hot *maître* boat. *d'hôtel*

For the butter, take two ounces of *butter* fresh Brittany, mix into it the juice of half a good lemon, and a dessertspoonful of finely chopped parsley, a pinch of white pepper, and half a saltspoonful of salt ; form the pat with the butter-bat, and use as required ; excellent with cutlets, &c.

Assuming that the remains of a pair of fowls

3

used at dinner the night previously are available, the following may be done : cut the birds up, neatly separating the thighs from the drum-
8. *Devilled* sticks, and dividing the backs in the
fowl ; chut- usual manner. Shred an onion very
ney sauce finely ; melt half an ounce of butter
(Indian). in a frying-pan, and fry the former till brown. Having meanwhile sprinkled the pieces of fowl with curry powder, and a dust of fine salt, put them into the pan with the butter and onions, turning them about to prevent burning. When the butter seems almost absorbed, turn the fowl and the onions with it into a hot dish. The operation after the pieces of fowl are put in should be conducted over a low fire, the object being to heat the meat thoroughly, and to serve it and the onions as dry as possible without burning. The onions can be brushed off if objected to before serving.

For the sauce : melt a quarter of an ounce of butter in a small saucepan, stir in a quarter of an ounce of flour ; when blended well add a teacupful of gravy, or broth, mix, and put in a dessertspoonful of Harvey sauce, the same of mushroom ketchup, a teaspoonful of chilli vinegar, and a dessertspoonful of good chutney. For additional heat, a teaspoonful of finely chopped skin of green chillies may be added, carefully omitting the seeds. Boil, strain, and serve with the fowl as hot as possible.

Cut six squares of bread a quarter of an inch thick and large enough to hold a poached egg each. Fry these crisply and brown, and keep them hot. Pass sufficient lean ham through the mincing machine to yield a top-dressing for each "toast"; warm the mince in a small saucepan over a low fire, with half an ounce of butter, *9. Ham toast, with poached eggs.* and moisten it with a spoonful of gravy or melted glaze. Keep this in the hot saucepan in the *bain-marie* while you poach six eggs; when they are ready, spread the mince on the fried bread, and place a poached egg on the surface of each, having trimmed the edges of the whites neatly all round. Send in quite hot.

MENU IV.

HAVING procured a nice haddock the previous day, stuff it with veal stuffing, and keep it in a cold place during the night. In the *10. Fresh* morning, when wanted for breakfast, *haddock,* egg, and strew a thin layer of raspings *anchovy butter.* over the fish, butter a fire-proof dish large enough to hold it, sprinkle a layer of chopped parsley over the bottom of the dish, and lay the fish upon it. Now set the Dutch oven in front of the fire, slip the dish into it, pour a few drops of butter-melted over, and watch the fish for a few minutes ; try with a skewer if tender, and draw the dish back as soon as that occurs. Serve the fish steaming hot in the dish in which it was dressed with a pat of anchovy butter melting over it.

For anchovy butter *see* No. 7, and proceed in the same manner, mixing into the butter two pounded anchovies instead of the parsley and lemon juice. In a hurry, a good substitute may be made by melting an ounce of butter, and stirring into it a dessertspoonful of Moir's *anchovy vinegar*, an excellent preparation too little known and used.

For breakfast it will be found very time-saving if, for these cutlets, part of the best end of a neck of mutton were *slightly* roasted the previous day. On the morning re- 11. *Mut-ton cutlets* quired, with a sharp knife and meat- saw each little chop can easily be *with broiled* detached, trimmed, and then be either *mush-* broiled, or breaded and fried, as may be *rooms.* desired. Serve the cutlets on a hot dish, accompanied by broiled mushrooms in a hot *entrée* dish.

Prepare the buttered eggs as described in No. 3, and serve them hot from the stewpan upon a bed of tomatoes dressed as follows :—

Choose six moderately sized tomatoes ; 12. *But-tered eggs* blanch them in scalding water for three *with to-* minutes to facilitate the removal of the *matoes.* skin, which having been done, take a small stewpan, put half an ounce of butter into it with one finely sliced half-ounce shallot ; fry till beginning to turn golden, then empty into the pan the whole of the tomatoes sliced thinly , stir round, and add a teaspoonful of coarsely ground black pepper (fresh from a table-mill for choice), a saltspoonful of powdered dry *basil*, and one of salt. Continue the stirring for ten minutes over a fairly brisk fire to prevent catching, and the tomatoes will be ready. A tablespoonful of white sauce, or the yolk of a raw egg should be stirred in—off the fire—before final dishing up. It is quite unnecessary to pass this through the sieve. People fond of Continental cookery can direct that one clove of garlic be stewed with the tomatoes, uncut, to be picked out before serving.

MENU V.

THIS is a sort of fricassee. I presume that half
(say a pound) a nice-sized brill has been left the
previous evening.   Detach all the meat
from the bones, take the latter, and put   13. *Molé*
them, with the skin and trimmings, an   *of brill*
onion sliced, salt, six peppercorns, and a   *(Indian)*.
little mace, into a small stewpan, cover with the
" boilings " (saved when the fish was first dressed),
and boil, then simmer for a quarter of an hour ;
drain ; put the broth thus obtained in a bowl
handy.   Meanwhile, when this was simmering,
slice a shallot in thin rings, also a bit of garlic
the size of a pea, fry these till yellow in an ounce
of butter, dredge in an ounce of rice flour and
teaspoonful of grated green ginger ; slowly now
add the warm fish-broth by degrees, and a table-

spoonful of desiccated cocoanut (as sold for puddings) with a teaspoonful of lemon juice ; let the
sauce come to the boil, simmer for five minutes,
colour it with a teaspoonful of turmeric, and
then strain it through the block-tin strainer over
the pieces of fish, which should have been placed
ready in a stewpan to receive the moistening.
Now gently warm up over a slow fire, garnish
with strips of finely cut green skin of chilli, dish
upon a hot dish, and serve steaming.

Boiled rice, if liked, may accompany the *Molé*,
as it does in India (*see* No. 20).

This should be almost wholly prepared overnight. Pass as much cold beef as will yield
ten tablespoonfuls of mince through
14. *Minced* the mincer. Take one ounce of maca-
beef, with
macaroni. roni, or better still, the remains of a
dish of macaroni *au gratin* or *à*
l'Italienne left from dinner. If the former, it
must of course be boiled. Take half a pint of
broth, thicken and flavour it as recommended in
No. 5. Put the mince into it, and set it in a
cold larder ; also put away the cooked macaroni.
In the morning all you have to do is to butter a
fire-proof baking dish, and fill it with mince and
cut-up macaroni, diluting the whole with a little
more gravy or broth, and shaking over the surface a layer of finely powdered crumbs and grated
cheese in half-and-half proportions. Heat this

thoroughly and send it up, in its own dish, upon
a folded napkin.

Arrange six nicely poached eggs upon six
squares of crisp, well-buttered toast.
Put a pat of *maître d'hôtel* butter upon 15. *Eggs à*
the top of each egg the size of a shilling, *la maître d'hôtel.*
and send them up with the butter
melting over them.   For the butter, *see* No. 7.

MENU VI.

A DOZEN smelts of moderate size will yield a nice dish for six. Egg and crumb them with finely sifted stale crumbs, and fry them one by one in very hot fat, drain on blotting-paper, and send them dry and crisp upon a fish-paper, with slices of lemon for garnish. If fried without colouring overnight they will be all the crisper when fried again in the morning.

16. Fried smelts.

Make sure when you order a grill that it is *grilled—i.e.*, done on the gridiron. Grills are too often cooked in the frying-pan, and are unsatisfactory in consequence (*see* No. 29). Besides this, mark the difference between a grill and a "devil"; the

17. Grilled partridge, with potato chips.

26

former need not necessarily be highly seasoned
or strongly peppered. The remains of four partridges of which part of the breasts alone have
been used will give a nice dish of grill ; let
them be neatly cut up, then butter the pieces,
sprinkle them with salt and black or white
pepper, and cook them on the gridiron, which
should be warmed and buttered to receive them.
Dish them, piled up, in a hot *entrée* dish, and
send a plate of potato chips with them. For
chips, remember you use raw potato sliced
thinly and evenly, dried carefully, and then
boiled, as it were, in very hot fat. The pan
should be deep and not wide, so as to ensure a
bath of fat ; not too many chips should be done
at a time ; do them in relays, drain, dry on a hot
cloth in front of the fire and serve. For cutting
chips an even thickness, Woolf and Co.'s " vegetable slicer " is a most handy instrument.

Œufs à l'Indienne are *poached* eggs smothered
with a thickish curry sauce, and are not to be
confounded with curried eggs. Prepare
six squares of fried bread as in No. 9, 18. *Eggs*
lay a nicely poached egg upon each of *à l'Indi-*
them, and send them up at once with *enne.*
the following sauce poured evenly over them :
Shred one shallot very finely, fry the slices in
one ounce of butter, or clarified dripping, over a
low fire till turning a pale brown ; then mix

with them a dessertspoonful of curry *paste* and
a dessertspoonful of curry *powder ;* mix, fry at
least for five minutes, and stir in a teaspoonful of rice flour ; dilute the jam-like paste now
formed with broth or milk by degrees, stirring
over a moderate fire till you have about a pint of
liquid, add to this a dessertspoonful of desiccated
cocoanut, a teaspoonful of sweetish chutney, with
a small teaspoonful of salt. Let the sauce boil ;
skim off the scum, simmer for ten minutes, and
then pass through the pointed strainer over the
eggs. The English practice of spoiling all pre-
parations of curries with sliced apples, green
gooseberries, and other acids, should be carefully avoided : there is ample sub-acid in all
good curry *paste*—viz., tamarind.   In India it
is not the custom to use acid adjuncts beyond
this, or a little lime juice. This sauce can of
course be made on the previous day.

MENU VII.

THE mackerel must of course be split, laid open, and broiled. I recommend this sauce—a good one for all fatty fishes : Proceed as usual to make a breakfastcupful of melted butter sauce ; when nice and smooth, stir in a tablespoonful of C. F. Buckle's "horse-radish zest," a pungent and well-flavoured composition very little known. The yolk of a raw egg—stirred in off the fire— is an improvement.

19.
Broiled mackerel.

Having peeled, trimmed, and cleaned a dozen fairly large mushrooms, put them (overnight) to simmer gently in the curry sauce described for the eggs in No. 18 for half an hour. Keep in a china dish during the night, warm up, without actual boiling, in the morning, and serve in a hot *entrée* dish.

For the rice there is only *one* method, easily learnt. Having cleaned and sifted the rice—say six ounces—prepare a large vessel of boiling water, a gallon not too much, put into the water a dessertspoonful of salt, and the juice of half a lemon to preserve the whiteness of the grains. When the water is at a gallop—*fully boiling*—throw in the rice, and stir it round with a wooden spoon ; watch the clock for ten minutes, stirring every now and then ; after ten minutes, test a few grains by pinching them between the finger and thumb ; as soon as soft, probably in twelve or thirteen minutes according to the size of the grains, stop the boiling instantly by a dash of cold water, immediately remove the vessel, and drain off every drop of the water from the rice, returning the latter to the now dry, hot pot in which it was boiled. Shake well, replace this upon the hot plate, or put it in front of the fire (a moderate heat required), and cover the rice with a folded cloth—do not use the lid—shake the vessel now and then, and after ten minutes' rest the rice will be fit to serve. The last process is necessary to dry and disintegrate the grains.

20. *Mushroom curry—rice.*

N.B.—Never *soak* rice before boiling, or put it into *cold* water, as some advise.

Spread an ounce of butter on a fire-proof dish sufficiently presentable to send to table ; sprinkle a thin dusting of salt and pepper over the surface, break six eggs carefully into *21. Eggs* the dish, dust a fine layer of salt over *in the dish.* them, and set the dish on the hot plate with brisk heat beneath ; pass the salamander over the surface of the eggs, so as to give heat above as well as below the dish, and in about four minutes, when the whites are set, the eggs will be ready. A dusting of finely grated cheese may be given over the eggs before serving if approved ; send up in the dish in which they were cooked.

To obtain the appearance called *au miroir* the salt should only be sprinkled over the whites, and a teaspoonful of butter melted should be poured over the yolks. This can be set in the oven.

MENU VIII.

To about a pound of any cold fish left at dinner cut up into a coarse mince, add four ounces of crumbs soaked in fish-boilings or stock, blend together, moistening with a break-fastcupful of warm sauce (that remaining after dinner should thus be used), with the yolk of an egg mixed into it. Stir the mixture over a low fire to thicken, then spread it upon a dish to get cold and set during the night. The mixture should be about half an inch thick when thus set. In the morning cut out of it as many cutlets as you can with a cutter ; egg and bread-crumb them, and fry in boiling fat as explained for smelts in No. 16. Serve with a breakfastcupful of ordinary white sauce with this flavouring, a tablespoonful of Harvey sauce, a dessertspoonful of mushroom ketchup, and a teaspoonful of anchovy sauce.

22. Fish cutlets.

32

Either broil the kidneys *à la brochette* (*see* No. 2) or crumb them, broiling four minutes on each side. For the sauce : thicken half a pint of gravy or stock with a quarter of an ounce of butter and a quarter of an ounce of flour, stirring in a tablespoonful of mushroom ketchup and a teaspoonful of anchovy vinegar (*see* No. 10). Next slice up two tomatoes, boil up in the sauce, simmer for ten minutes, seasoning with a saltspoonful of salt and one of roughly ground fresh black pepper, then pass through the pointed tin strainer into a hot sauce boat. To this sauce *may* be added a mince composed of ham, mushroom, and parsley—a dessertspoonful each of the two former, and a teaspoonful of the latter, both of course previously cooked.

23. Veal kidneys à l'Italienne.

Make the *omelettes* as described in No. 6, omitting the herbs ; having cut up four fairly sized mushrooms, or a quarter of a pound of any size, and fried the mince in butter immediately beforehand. Keep the mince hot in the pan in which it was cooked, and as soon as one *omelette* is ready to turn into the hot dish, rapidly pour half of the former over the surface of the latter, which will envelop it as it rolls over from the pan to the dish. Repeat the process with the second *omelette*.

24. Omelette with mushrooms.

4

MENU IX.

Fish Pudding.

Cold meat cutlets, with grilled bacon.

Eggs with anchovies.

Wholemeal cakes.

PICK about a pound of cold cooked fish free from bones, skin, &c. Make with the latter and any of the fish-boilings saved (flavoured with one onion sliced, pepper, salt, and a pinch of powdered mace), about a pint of nice broth ; strain this. Next take of cold cooked potato the same bulk as you have of fish, and boil three eggs hard. Measure two ounces of butter and a tablespoonful of minced parsley. Have the sauce left at dinner preserved for this. Empty the fish and potato into a roomy bowl and mash them together, adding the cold sauce, and moistening with the broth to get the mixture to work easily. Crush the hard-boiled eggs with a fork and add them to the fish and potato ; mix a teaspoonful of salt with one of white

25. Fish pudding.

pepper, and a saltspoonful of mace, and dust the
seasoning into the mixture ; stir in the parsley
and butter, and lastly a tablespoonful of milk.
All being blended, put the pudding into a buttered mould, put this into a pan with boiling
water round it half the depth of the mould, heat
it thoroughly in the oven, and then turn it out
carefully ; shake some fine crust raspings over
it, and send to table. If liked, ordinary melted
butter and anchovy sauce may accompany in a
boat.

These are to be made with any cold cooked
meats—overnight—in the same manner as the
fish cutlets described in No. 22. Serve *26. Cold*
them with fried parsley and tiny rolls *meat cut-*
of crisply fried bacon. Any brown *lets, with*
sauce left at the previous evening's *grilled*
dinner may be warmed up to ac- *bacon.*
company.

Prepare six squares of crisply fried bread, as in
No. 9, butter them with anchovy butter (*see*
No.10). Put a nicely poached egg on
each square thus buttered, and lay two *27. Eggs*
little strips of anchovies, cut from the *with an-*
filleted fish, crosswise, on the top of *chovies.*
each egg.

MENU X.

Fried soles—capers butter.

Devilled turkey.

Eggs with vegetable marrow.

Tea-cake, not sweetened.

FOR breakfast it is desirable to cut the soles

28. *Fried* into pieces, across—say two inches wide;
soles— to egg and bread-crumb these, and fry
capers them as explained for smelts (No. 16).
butter. Serve after draining and drying in the
same manner.

For capers butter *see* No. 7, and proceed in
the way therein given, mixing into the butter a
dessertspoonful of well-pounded capers instead of
the parsley and lemon.

ON GRILLS AND DEVILS.—For breakfast few
dishes are more popular than these, while the

excellence of devilled bones for a *very*
29. *Devil-* late supper need hardly be mentioned.
led turkey. The utensil necessary for their preparation is the *gridiron.* Many cooks spoil their

36

grills by using the frying-pan, for though the
bones may be served in a wet as well as in a dry
form, they must be themselves broiled over a
clear fire. The meat attached to the bone,
whether a turkey leg, or the bones of a saddle
of mutton, must be scotched with a sharp knife
criss-crosswise, and bountifully peppered with
this seasoning :—one teaspoonful of Nepaul
pepper, one teaspoonful black pepper coarsely
ground, two teaspoonfuls of salt, mixed well
together. Following these proportions a bottle
of "grill-seasoning" can be made, and labelled
for use when required. Mix your mustard for
your grill with Worcester sauce instead of water
or vinegar, and if you want "the very devil" of
a grill, add to it six drops of *Tabasco*. Smear
this over the seasoned bones, rub the bars of the
gridiron with butter, lay the bones thereon, and
grill them. If here and there they scorch a little,
so much the better. Serve without delay "from the
grid to the plate," so to speak. This is a dry grill.
For a wet grill proceed exactly as directed for the
dry, but roll the bones, after broiling them, in a
sauté pan for a few minutes in this sauce :—

DEVIL SAUCE. — Take a breakfastcupful of
gravy, or a broth made from scraps, and half
an ounce of glaze or a teaspoonful of Brand's
essence ; put this into a saucepan and add to it
a tablespoonful of hot yet sweetish bottled chutney, a tablespoonful of mustard mixed with

Worcester sauce, a tablespoonful of mushroom ketchup, a tablespoonful of Marsala, half a teaspoonful of red-currant jelly, and a teaspoonful of chilli vinegar; heat all together to melt the jelly and blend the ingredients, then strain, and thicken with half an ounce of butter, and half an ounce of flour, heat this up to boiling point in a frying-pan, and roll the grilled bones in it off the fire, serving them quickly with the rest of the sauce in the pan poured over them.

A moderately sized young vegetable marrow, cold boiled, and six hard-boiled eggs will be wanted for this dish. Cut the marrow into fillets freed from seeds, one and a half inch long, three-quarters of an inch wide, and the depth of the marrow; slice each egg in half longitudinally; take the water in which the marrow was boiled (an onion boiled with it would have been an improvement), and using an ounce of butter and one of flour proceed to thicken it; season with a saltspoonful of black pepper, half one of powdered mace, and a teaspoonful of salt: add a tablespoonful of chopped parsley and a teaspoonful of chopped chervil. Now arrange the eggs and fillets of marrow neatly in a hot *entrée* dish, add a tablespoonful of milk, with which one raw yolk has been well mixed, to the sauce off the fire, and pour it over the fillets and eggs, steaming hot.

30. Eggs with vegetable marrow.

MENU XI.

———

FOR these fritters, which will be found very
tasty, about half a pound of any cold fish, such
as whiting, fresh haddock, gurnard, or
plaice, that will pound easily, will be   31. *Fish
enough.   A batter must be made as *fritters.*
follows : Beat up the yolks of four eggs with
two tablespoonfuls of beer, one tablespoonful of
salad oil, and five tablespoonfuls of water.
Having pounded the fish well, mix it with the
beaten eggs, &c., and add a saltspoonful of salt,
and enough flour to bring the mixture to the
consistency of a thick batter. Put the frying
fat into a small but deep pan, and while it is heating, beat up the whites of the eggs to a stiff
froth, add this to the batter the last thing, and
then, when the fat is *very* hot, proceed to put

about a tablespoonful of the mixture into it at a time. The batter will frizzle up at the moment of contact, and assume an irregular shape. Each fritter having been cooked a rich golden brown, should be drained with a perforated slice and laid on a hot cloth to dry before dishing. Pile the fritters on a hot dish, and serve with slices of lemon.

About three-quarters of a pint of good broth or gravy, six kidneys, and six medium-sized mushrooms are wanted, and the preparation should take place on the previous day. Take a stewpan and commence by thickening the gravy in the usual manner, then add the kidneys cut into slices ; stew them very slowly ; if allowed to boil they will be as tough as leather. After they have simmered for about half an hour put in the mushrooms, with a teaspoonful of salt and one of black pepper, and half a sherry-glass of mushroom ketchup ; continue the stewing now till the kidneys are done, then put the stew into a china dish to keep till the next day. In the morning put it into a stewpan, and if any additional liquid is necessary add a little milk ; warm up in the *bain-marie*. When ready to serve, stir in a dessertspoonful of Marsala.

32. Kidneys stewed with mushrooms.

Boil six eggs for exactly four minutes ; put

them at once into cold water ; when cold carefully remove the shells ; the eggs will be soft to
the touch, the yolks inside them not
having hardened.   Have ready a pint
of nice white sauce seasoned with
pepper and spiced salt ; flavour this
with a tablespoonful (mixed) of finely chopped
tarragon, parsley, chives, and chervil, and sharpen
it with a dessertspoonful of anchovy vinegar ; put
the eggs on a hot dish, and pour the sauce
boiling hot over them.   Serve.

33. *Eggs
" mollets "
with " ra-
vigote."*

MENU XII.

Fish custard puddings.

Purée of grouse in scallops.

Eggs with mushrooms.

Scones.

THESE are tasty little fish puddings very easily made. Any cold fish will do. Choose six *dariole* moulds, fluted or plain; butter them, and sprinkle a layer of finely minced, dry parsley over this lining. Make enough ordinary thick custard to fill the moulds about half full each, seasoning it with salt and pepper instead of sugar. Pick the cold fish free from bones and skin, and cut it up into a coarse mince; dust into this a saltspoonful of spiced pepper; fill the moulds loosely with this, and then pour the custard over each, allowing time for it to settle well, and adding more custard till the moulds are filled; put a round of buttered paper over each of them, and place them in a *sauté* pan with enough boiling water round them to poach them nicely. When set, pick off the papers, and turn the moulded custards

34. Fish custard puddings.

42

out. A saltspoonful of anchovy sauce may be stirred into the custard before filling the moulds if liked. Excellent with cold salmon.

Pick and mince the meat from the birds overnight, and make as much well-flavoured broth from the bones as you can. This having been prepared, the work the next 35. *Purée* morning will be quickly done. Simply *of grouse* thicken the broth, flavour it with half *in scallops.* a teaspoonful of red-currant jelly and a dessertspoonful of Marsala, season it with salt, and a teaspoonful of spiced pepper. Then stir in the mince, keep it hot in the *bain-marie* while you butter six scallop shells, into which, when ready, pour the mince, shake a layer of pounded crumbs over the surface of each, and heat well in the oven or Dutch oven ; brown the crumbs with a salamander, and send up.

On six squares of fried bread place six nicely poached eggs, pouring over each about a tablespoonful of this sauce. Stew four medium mushrooms, or a quarter of 36. *Eggs* a pound of small ones, in milk, having *with mush-* first cleaned them carefully and cut *rooms.* them up into a coarse mince ; season with pepper and salt ; when ready stir in a tablespoonful of milk with which a raw yolk has been mixed, off the fire, and use as directed.

MENU XIII.

Fried flounders, tomato butter

Curry cutlets, chutney sauce

Eggs with green peas.

Bannocks.

PROCURE enough flounders for the party, and fry them as explained for smelts (No. 16) ; serve 37. *Fried* drained dry on a hot dish lined with a *flounders,* fish-paper, and this butter on a plate : *tomato* To two ounces of Brittany butter add *butter.* a good tablespoonful of French tomato *conserve* (it is much thicker than sauce), season if necessary, and work them together with the butter-bat. A little of this should be taken as an adjunct with the fish, and allowed to melt over it.

Prepare overnight enough minced veal, mutton, lamb, or even mixed meats—partly of fowl and mutton, for instance—as will suffice for half a dozen good cutlets. Dilute this with the sauce given for No. 18, using gravy or broth instead of

44

milk, and stirring into it the yolks of two raw
eggs ; thicken gently over a low fire, carefully
avoiding boiling, then turn the mixture
out upon a dish, patting it into a rect-
angular shape, a quarter of an inch thick,
with a wooden spoon ; set this aside in a
cool place for the night. In the morning it will
be quite firm ; cut out of it six or eight neat cutlets with your cutter, bread-crumb and fry them
a golden brown, and serve with them the sauce
given for No. 8.

38. *Curry
cutlets,
chutney
sauce.*

If fresh peas are not available—those left from
the previous evening's dinner, for instance—a
very nice dish for a change can be
made with a small tin of French *petits
pois* in this way : Open the tin, and
placing a block-tin strainer over a
bowl, empty the contents of the tin into it,
drain thoroughly, catching all the liquid : next,
with half an ounce of butter and half an ounce
of flour make a thickening at the bottom of a
small stewpan over a low fire ; when smooth add
the liquid from the tin, stir well, increasing the
heat and adding a coffeecupful of milk ; bring
to the boil, and when nice and thick put in the
peas with a saltspoonful of salt, one of sugar, and
half one of white pepper. Now set the stewpan
in the *bain-marie.* When required turn the
peas with their sauce into a hot *entrée* dish, and

39. *Eggs
with green
peas.*

lay on the surface six nicely poached eggs, gar·
nishing with sippets of fried bread.　A spoonful
of cream may of course be added just before
dishing the peas.

MENU XIV.

ABSTINENCE.

Khitchri (Indian).

Macaroni à la Livornaise.

Eggs in white sauce.

Sally Lunns.

———

THIS dish, from which the so-called "kedge-ree" of English cookery books was doubtless taken, was originally a dish of rice cooked with butter and an Indian pea called *dál*, but now it may either be composed of cold cooked fresh fish, or of salt fish that has been soaked and either boiled or fried. Choose which you prefer—about one pound will be enough—and with a fork divide it into small pieces. Boil six ounces of rice, as explained for No. 20. These preparations can be made overnight. Boil three eggs hard, and with a fork crush them, whites and yolks together, to a coarse mince. Melt over a low fire three ounces of butter, and fry a very finely minced shallot therein till it is a yellow colour ;

40. *Khit chri* (*Indian*).

now stir in the rice, using a wooden spoon, and
the pieces of fish, season with pepper and salt
and sufficient *turmeric* (about a teaspoonful) *to
tint the rice a nice light yellow colour ;* lastly,
shake into the mixture the crushed hard-boiled
eggs, and empty the whole into a very hot dish.

N.B. — Both onions and turmeric may be
omitted, if it be desired, without prejudice to the
mixture generally.

Boil six ounces of macaroni ; stew six medium-
sized mushrooms in milk, and season them with
pepper and salt. Make a breakfastcupful of tomato *purée.* Put a layer
of the macaroni in a well-buttered,
fire-proof baking dish, moisten it with
some of the *purée,* put a little of the stewed
mushroom over that, and then another layer of
macaroni, finally dusting the surface over with a
layer of grated cheese. Bake, and send up very hot.

41. *Maca-
roni à la
Livornaise.*

Six hard-boiled eggs sliced in halves longitudinally, a pint of white sauce, seasoning of pepper,
salt, and powdered dried herbs. A
tablespoonful of milk with the yolk
of an egg beaten up with it. Season
the pieces of egg, and arrange them on
a hot *entrée* dish ; heat the sauce very hot, stir
into it, off the fire, the tablespoonful of milk,
&c., and pour it over the eggs. Serve.

42. *Eggs
in white
sauce.*

MENU XV.

THIS method of serving fish for breakfast is a *spécialité* at the Bombay and Madras clubs. I recommend its trial with brill because that fish is more like the Indian
"pomfret" than any other English
fish ; at the same time the system is applicable to any kind of flat fish or slices of fish, from salmon downwards. Choose a fish of about a pound and a half or two pounds. Take the flesh from the bones as you do the fillets of a sole, trim them neatly, and dry them with a cloth. Now prepare a fire of cocoanut fibre (procurable at Treloar and Sons, 70, Ludgate Hill) ; when damped it makes a great volume of smoke ; place the gridiron over the fire, but well in the smoke, butter the fish fillets on both sides, lay them

43. Smoked brill.

side by side on the gridiron, covering them, as they are cooking in the vapour, with the lid of a tin fish-kettle to concentrate the smoke. In about ten minutes the fish will turn a rich warm brown on the side nearer the fire ; then turn it and smoke the other side, which will take about five minutes. The fillets can now be served with any plain sharp sauce. The process can be conducted in an ordinary fire-grate if the kitchen range be a closed one, and in smoke produced from damp clean straw, or shavings laid on a wood fire.

Breaded kidneys. Six kidneys will do for the party. Proceed as laid down for kidney *à la brochette* (No. 2). Skewer them, 44. *Mutton kidneys bread- crumbed.* omitting the bacon ; egg and bread-crumb them, boil over a bright, clear fire, and serve on the skewers, garnished with crisply fried curls of bacon. The sauce given for No. 23 will do.

Choose six little scallop shells, or mince-pie patty-pans ; put into each a piece of butter the 45. *Eggs in cases.* size of a cobnut, and a teaspoonful of minced "*fines herbes*"—*i.e.*, chopped mushroom, chopped parsley, and finely chopped stem of fresh green onion, or chives, the proportion of the mixture being equal measure of the first two ingredients to one-third of the measure of the last. Warm the shells over the hot plate, and when the butter has melted break an egg into each of them ; shake a layer of finely sifted bread-crumb over the surface, and keep over moderate heat till the eggs set, then brown them with the salamander, and serve.

MENU XVI.

Fricassee of cod and oysters.

Rissoles of ham and chicken.

Omelettes with tomatoes.

Buttered toast.

PRESUMING that the fish for dinner has been cod and oysters, a fricassee of what remains of them will be nice for breakfast the next day. Pick the meat in firm, flaky pieces from the bones; put the former aside, while with the latter and the fish-boilings you make a strong broth, using an onion and seasoning to assist the operation; strain and turn this into a moderately thick white sauce, and flavour it with a teaspoonful of essence of anchovy. Now arrange the cod in a stewpan, moisten it with the sauce, and heat it gently up in the *bain-marie* to steaming point; lastly, add the remaining oyster sauce, and empty the fricassee into a hot *entrée* dish. Or the mixture may be put into a fire-proof dish, dusted over with raspings, and baked.

46. Fricassee of cod and oysters.

These can be made the previous day, and can be easily heated for breakfast. Having prepared your *salpicon*, or coarse mince of ham and chicken (a quarter of a pound of the former to half a pound of the latter), with a good thick sauce, in which the yolks of two raw eggs have been mixed, roll out rather thinly half a pound of nice puff paste, and out of it cut six or eight circular pieces four inches in diameter. Put a tablespoonful of the *salpicon* upon each of these, turn over the paste, and wet and pinch the edges all round. The *rissoles*—now of a semi-circular or cocked-hat shape—should be plunged into very hot fat and fried fast. The next day let them be heated on a hot napkin in the Dutch oven. Fried parsley is the usual garnish, and a boat of tomato sauce a good accompaniment. Please note that bread-crumbed mixtures of meats (*croquettes*) are not *rissoles*, though often called by that name.

47. Rissoles of soles of ham and chicken.

I will now give you the variation in *omelette*-making promised in No. 6. Select a roomy *omelette* pan ; see that it is clean and dry ; break, one after another, five eggs, carefully separating the yolks from the whites ; put these into separate basins, whisk the whites to a stiffish froth, and mix the yolks well with a fork. Place the

48. Omelettes with tomatoes.

pan on the fire with half an ounce of butter ; let this get hot as for the *omelette* in No. 6, and when it is ready quickly amalgamate the contents of the two bowls and pour the mixture into the pan ; let it alone for three minutes, shake, and turn the *omelette* over upon a bed of tomatoes, as explained for No. 12. The minced herbs mentioned in No. 6 can be stirred in with the yolks if liked, and a teaspoonful of salt should be mixed with them also.

If you possess a glazing-iron, heat it, and pass it closely above the surface of the *omelette* while the bottom is setting. In any case the upper side remains frothy, and is buried as the *omelette* laps over in dishing. It is as light as a *soufflé*, and sweet *omelettes* thus cooked are excellent.

N.B.—Owing to the frothiness of the mixture a large pan is necessary. If this be not available it will be safer to divide the mixture, putting it into two bowls separately, and to cook each independently. The fire should not be too fierce.

MENU XVII.

Sardines au gratin.

Crêpinettes of mixed game.

Eggs with prawn butter.

Devilled biscuits.

ACCIDENTS may sometimes occur when. it may be found very convenient to fall back on the tin of sardines. On such an occasion this will be found a useful recipe :—Care-fully lift out a dozen sardines one by one, lay them on a medium-sized joint *49. Sardines au gratin.* dish, separately ; tip the dish up, and pour gently over the little fish a stream of very hot water, to carry off the fishy oil ; pour this off once or twice, drain, and the sardines will be clean. Now choose a flat *gratin* dish, or fire-proof baking dish, butter it liberally, and strew over the butter a goodly sprinkling of the "*fines herbes*" given in No. 45. Lay the sardines on this bed, putting a saltspoonful of the *herbes* on each of them, dredge lightly over all a dusting of fine salt and white pepper mixed together, pour a few drops of melted butter over them, and a thin layer of crust raspings ; heat thoroughly in the Dutch oven, and serve.

Although the term is usually applied to pre-parations of minced meats, wrapped in pig's 50. *Crêpi-* caul, crumbed, and fried, a *crêpinette* *nettes of* is literally a thing frizzled, or made *mixed* crisp, and pancakes are very useful as *game.* envelopes for *salpicon* of any kind. Make two or three ordinary thin pancakes plainly seasoned with salt and pepper instead of sugar, and a sprinkling of finely chopped parsley. Let them get cold, then cut out of them a dozen pieces five inches long and four wide ; lay these on a floured pastry board, brush a coating of white of egg over the upper surface, upon this put a good tablespoonful of hare, grouse, partridge, or mixed game *purée*, mois-tened with a thick brown sauce, as given for No. 35, and roll the pancake up as you would a sausage-roll. A very thin slice of cold cooked bacon may be laid over each of the *crêpinettes* first, and the mince over it. This much can be done the evening before. To prepare the *crêpi-nettes* for the table : Egg and bread-crumb them, and either fry them in boiling fat, or bake them. Curls of fried bacon can accom-pany them.

Poach the eggs, lay them on squares of fried bread, and send them up with a pat of this butter melting over them: Choose six *51. Eggs* nice boiled prawns; pick them; pour a *with* jug of cold water over the shells and *prawn* meat also ; when quite clean pound *butter.* meat and shells together in a stone mortar, using an ounce of butter to assist the pounding. When thoroughly pounded pass the paste through a hair-sieve into a bowl of cold water, skim it off the water, drain it, and add it to another ounce of butter with the butter-bat, seasoning, it with a saltspoonful of salt, white pepper, and mace blended. Shrimps may be substituted for prawns.

Fried plaice, shrimp butter.

Fowl (or turkey) marinaded.

Eggs in bread sauce.

Tea-cake—not sweetened.

SKIN and trim a plaice, dividing it into fillets two inches and a half long, and one and a half wide :

52. *Fried plaice, shrimp butter.* marinade them all night, as recommended in No. 73. In the morning wipe them dry, egg, bread-crumb, and fry these as explained for smelts (No. 16). Serve on a neat fish-paper garnished with slices of lemon, and send in with them a little plate of shrimp butter made as explained for prawn butter (No. 51).

Cut up a chicken or half a large fowl into neat pieces as for fricassee. Put these overnight into a soup-plate in a *marinade* composed of two table-spoonfuls of salad oil, two of vinegar, one finely sliced shallot, one inch length of celery shredded, a dozen peppercorns, a sprig of parsley chopped, and a saltspoonful of salt. In the morning drain the pieces, dry them, prepare a bath of boiling fat, dip the pieces in frying *53. Fowl (or turkey)* batter (No. 116), fry a golden brown ; *marinaded.* drain, dry, and pile upon a napkin.

Flavour a pint of milk as you would for bread sauce—*i.e.*, cut in quarters and blanch a three-ounce onion in boiling water for five minutes, drain the pieces and simmer *54. Eggs* them in the milk with six cloves and *in bread sauce.* a saltspoonful of salt. When nicely flavoured turn the milk into a white sauce, with half an ounce of butter and the same of flour. Choose a large fire-proof baking dish, butter it, pour over the bottom of it a layer of the sauce at least a quarter of an inch deep ; over this strew a layer of pounded bread crumbs seasoned with salt, pepper, and mace blended. Put the dish in the oven for a few minutes to heat without boiling, take it out and slip into it carefully, without breaking one of them, six eggs ; dust a layer of very fine raspings over the surface, and return the dish to the oven just long enough for the eggs to set. Grated cheese may be mingled both with the crumbs and the raspings if liked.

MENU XIX.

SOAK and boil the haddocks (two required, if small) till the meat can be picked easily from *55. Dried* the bones and skin ; make a good pint *haddock,* of egg sauce slightly flavoured with *with egg* anchovy, arrange the picked haddock *sauce.* on a very hot dish, season it with a little salt and black pepper, pour the egg sauce, steaming hot, over it, and serve.

Impale the kidneys as described in No. 2, give them a broil for two minutes, then roll them on a dish, upon which you have spread *56. Devil-* a thin layer of made mustard ; now *led kidneys.* dust over the mustard-coated kidneys a good seasoning of salt and black pepper, and continue the broiling till they are done. Serve with the sauce given in No. 8.

Curried eggs differ from eggs *à l'Indienne* (No. 18), inasmuch as they are hard-boiled, while the latter are poached, and are simmered *in* the curry sauce, not merely *57. Curried eggs.* covered with it as the poached eggs
are. Boil overnight six eggs hard, slice them when cold in halves longitudinally, cut twelve nice fillets of cold cooked vegetable marrow or stewed cucumber, each piece to be about the size of one of the half eggs. Prepare a curry sauce as given for No. 18, put into it the eggs and pieces of marrow, and slowly heat them up to steaming point; let them rest all night thus prepared, and simply re-heat the dish in the morning. The curry will be far better if allowed thus to *marinade* for twelve hours in its own sauce. Fried ham or bacon may accompany.

MENU XX.

Lobster cutlets à la Turque.

Irish stew à la Wyvern.

Poached eggs with Italian sauce.

Barley meal scones.

EITHER fresh or tinned lobster may be used.
Take enough lobster to form, with an addition
of one-third of its bulk of panada,
58. *Lobster* about six or eight nice cutlets ; season
cutlets à la the mixture, after pounding and mixing
Turque.
it well, with salt, white pepper, and
mace blended ; moisten it over a low fire with
white sauce (in which the raw yolk of egg has
been mixed) for a few minutes to thicken, and let
it set firmly in a dish. Thus much having been
done overnight, proceed the next morning to
form the mixture into cutlets or balls and cook
in the manner described for No. 22. Rice *à la
Turque* should accompany—*i.e.,* " yellow rice "
thus prepared : Boil six ounces of rice according
to the directions for it in No. 20, then drain,

shake over it a teaspoonful of turmeric powder, mixing it well into the rice ; a dust of nutmeg may be also given. Pile the rice on the hot dish prepared for it, and arrange the cutlets or balls round it. If liked the sauce mentioned for No. 8 may accompany.

I adopt a slightly different way of making Irish stew, which I think may be liked. Take the best end of the neck of mutton, cut from a small-sized sheep and not 59. *Irish* too fat. Divide this into eight or ten *stew à la* equally sized cutlets, and put them into *Wyvern.* a large stewpan with eight ounces of onions, four of carrots, four ounces of turnip, and an ounce of celery, with a seasoning of salt and black pepper-corns. Bring once to the boil and then simmer slowly for an hour. When nicely done, and the meat quite tender, strain off the broth, and set it to get cold and throw up the fat ; put the cutlets on a dish, and the onions on another separately. Now peel and boil two and a half pounds of potatoes, which, when ready, drain and mash in their own hot saucepan, mashing the onions from the stew with them, and moistening the whole with enough of the now skimmed broth to bring the vegetables to the consistency of a good *purée.* If required, a little more salt and freshly ground black pepper seasoning can now be added. Next put the cutlets into a stewpan, add a spoonful or

two of the broth to the *purée* of potato and
onions, pour this over the meat, and slowly heat
up the stew to steaming point. Dish in this
way : arrange the cutlets in a row in a hot silver
dish, and mask them with the *purée*. Some add
milk or cream to Irish stew, but I do not think
it necessary. In my way you have all the flavour
of the mutton broth and *no grease*, while the
potato is creamy and free from lumps, with the
onion *there*, but not *en evidence*.

60. *Poached eggs, with Italian sauce.* Put six poached eggs on six squares
of fried bread, and pour enough of the
sauce given in No. 23 to cover each
nicely.

MENU XXI.

ABSTINENCE.

Fillets of sole, with shrimps,

Spaghetti à la Milanaise,

Omelette with artichokes.

Muffins.

HAVE a good-sized sole neatly filleted. Order the bones and trimmings to be sent in with the fish, and with them make a good fish *61. Fillets* broth. Also order half a pint of picked *of sole,* shrimps, mince them not too finely, *with* and season the mince with salt, white *shrimps.* pepper, and a pinch of mace. Lay the fillets on a board, brush the upper sides of them with white of egg, and spread over each a coating of the mince after having moistened it with a quarter of a pint of white sauce made with the fish broth and thickened with a raw egg. Roll up the fillets and poach them in the remaining broth to set the farce. Let them get cold. If thus prepared overnight they can be lightly floured or bread-crumbed and fried for breakfast, anchovy or shrimp butter accompanying.

6   65

Spaghetti seems more delicate than macaroni. Weigh six ounces of it and boil the spaghetti till tender,[1] then drain ; while hot, and in the same saucepan, quickly melt a couple of ounces of butter into it, stir it well about with a wooden spoon, flavour it with a teaspoonful of spiced pepper, and finish with three ounces of grated cheese ; stir all together vigorously, and then serve piled up on a hot dish, steaming.

62. Spaghetti à la Milanaise.

Cut six artichoke bottoms into six pieces each, toss them in chopped parsley and butter, seasoning with white pepper and salt ; make an *omelette* in either of the ways already explained. Dish as follows : Melt a pat of butter at the bottom of the hot *entrée* dish, put in the artichokes, upon them lay the *omelette*, and serve.

63. Omelette with artichokes.

[1] Boil macaroni or spaghetti exactly as you do rice (No. 20) for all ordinary purposes. It should be firm not pulpy.

MENU XXII.

CHOOSE two large or three medium whitings, untouched by the fishmonger. Have them simply trimmed and *scored—i.e.*, cuts about a quarter of an inch deep, made at two-inch intervals along both sides. Thus prepared they will lie *flat* on the *gratin* dish, not curled round in the manner invariably adopted by the fishmonger. Butter the baking dish well, sprinkle over its surface a saltspoonful of salt and one of white pepper, and dredge about two tablespoonfuls of fine raspings over all. Brush the whitings on one side with egg, and sprinkle over them some finely minced mushroom, put them in the dish with this side upwards, melt half an ounce of butter and moisten the surface of the mushrooms, sprinkle a layer of chopped parsley over that, and

64. *Whitings au gratin.*

two more tablespoonfuls of raspings, moisten
with a coffeecupful of broth, and set the dish
in the oven for ten or twelve minutes ; serve in
the same dish laid on a napkin.

N.B.—The mushroom is, of course, optional.

Pound well on the day previously seven ounces
of cold cooked chicken and five ounces of cold
lean ham, after first passing the meat
65. *Little* through the mincing machine ; incor-
moulds of porate with this six ounces of panada, one
ham and
chicken. ounce of butter, a saltspoonful of white
pepper, half one of mace, and a pinch of
salt ; mix all together with two well-beaten eggs,
and about two tablespoonfuls of thick white
sauce made with broth extracted from the bones
and trimmings of the chicken. Now butter six
or eight *dariole* moulds, shake a thin lining of
rasped crumbs over this, then proceed to fill the
little moulds with the mixture ; shake them down
well so that the latter may settle closely into them,
then with the back of a saltspoon scoop out a
hollow in each ; into these little cavities put a
teaspoonful of the sauce, and close them with
a cap of the mixture you took out, smoothing
over the surface with the blade of a dessert-knife
dipped in water. Now poach the little moulds
till set firmly, and put them in a cold place till
morning, when they can be gently warmed *en
bain-marie* and turned out.

Prepare six squares of hot buttered toast, cover each with a canopy of buttered eggs, and sprinkle a layer of finely rasped Hamburg or cold salt beef (red) over the top of each ; serve as hot as possible.

66. Buttered eggs with grated beef.

MENU XXIII

———————

STEEP a pound and a half of salt cod for six or eight hours in lukewarm water, changing it three times, finally leaving it in cold water for three hours longer. Put it on to boil in *cold* water; as soon as boiling ease off the fire, and let it simmer for five minutes, drain it, set it on a hot dish on a bed of nicely mashed potato, and pour a pint of well-made hard-boiled egg sauce over it. The potato should be worked more as a *purée* in the French way—that is, diluted with stock or milk until it can be *poured* out of the saucepan about the consistency of porridge.

67. Salt cod with egg sauce and potatoes.

Slice up about a pound or so of calf's liver lengthwise, about half an inch thick, season with

a seasoning composed of salt, white pepper, and
powdered dried herbs in equal portions, and a
saltspoonful of mace blended with it.

Melt four ounces of clarified dripping 68. *Calf's*
or veal suet in a frying-pan ; when this *liver à*
is hot put in the liver, fry for three *l'Itali-*
minutes on one side, then turn the *enne.*
slices and fry three minutes on the other side ;
take the slices out and lay them on a hot *entrée*
dish closely covered. Now put into the frying
fat one ounce of flour, work it well, add one shallot chopped small, a couple of mushrooms also
chopped, and enough broth to bring the sauce
to a nice consistency ; finally add a tablespoonful
of chopped parsley ; skim well, pour through a
pointed strainer over the liver, and serve.

Poach six eggs, and lay them on squares of
fried bread, and cover them with this sauce :
Half an ounce of butter, half an ounce 69. *Eggs*
of flour, and enough milk to make a *with*
rather thin sauce. Season with a salt- *shrimp*
spoonful of salt and black pepper *cream.*
blended, and stir in enough potted shrimps to
thicken the sauce well.

MENU XXIV.

Stewed fish.

Epigrams of mutton.

Eggs with Soubise sauce.

Sally Lunns.

———

FOR this choose any cheap yet *clean* fish—*i.e.*, not
"*fatty*," as herrings, mackerel, &c. ; about one
and a half pounds enough, have the
fish filleted if you wish, but ask that all
the "cuttings" may be sent with it.
With the latter, assisted by two or three onions,
a bit of celery, six peppercorns, a seasoning of
salt, a bunch of parsley and herbs, and a tablespoonful of grated *horseradish*, make a good fish
broth ; strain when quite done, and thicken,
then put the fillets into it, and simmer them till
they are cooked ; lastly, stir in the yolk of an
egg, off the fire ; dish on a hot dish, and serve.

70. *Stewed fish.*

Select about a pound and a half of breast of
mutton, cover it with cold water, and stew it,

with ordinary broth, vegetables, and seasoning,
till it is tender, then strain off the broth, take
out the mutton, remove the bones
(they will come out easily), sprinkle *71. Epi-*
some salt and pepper over the meat, *grams of*
and put it on a dish under a weight for *mutton.*
the night, setting the broth in a bowl. In the
morning cut the meat into convenient pieces ;
egg, bread-crumb them, and fry them a nice
colour in very hot fat ; dish on a hot dish, and
send this sauce with them : Take the fat off
the bowl of broth, put about half a pint of it
into a saucepan, colour it a nice brown with
browning, and mix into it a teaspoonful of red-
currant jelly, a tablespoonful of Harvey, one of
mushroom ketchup, a teaspoonful of anchovy
vinegar, and a dessertspoonful of Marsala. If the
fire be clear the pieces of mutton may be broiled
instead of being fried.

Prepare six " *œufs mollets* " (No. 33), put them
in a hot *entrée* dish, and pour over them a pint
of sauce Soubise—*i.e.*, three two-ounce
onions boiled till tender in milk or *72. Eggs*
broth, then passed through the sieve— *with Sou-*
heated up in the same liquid slightly *bise sauce.*
thickened with arrowroot, seasoned with pepper
and salt, and finished with a yolk of a raw egg
if liked. Prepare the sauce overnight.

MENU XXV.

Fried brill.

Salmis of game.

Devilled eggs.

Muffins.

ABOUT one pound and a half of filleted brill.
Parboil them overnight, and lay them, when
cold, in a *marinade* composed as
follows : Four tablespoonfuls of salad
oil, one of vinegar, an onion sliced in
rings, a tablespoonful of chopped parsley, one of
mixed green herbs, the peel of half a lemon, and
a teaspoonful of black pepper and salt blended.
In the morning take the fillets out of the *marinade*, wipe them, egg, bread-crumb, and fry them
as explained for smelts (No. 16).

73. Fried brill.

N.B.—*Maître d'hôtel* butter may accompany.

Although a true *salmis* should be made with

game which has been only partly cooked beforehand, a very eatable dish can be concocted out
of the remains of birds, provided that
they have not been over-roasted. Presuming, then, that you have some
remains of game—hare, grouse, black game,
or partridges—you can proceed in this way on
the evening before : Cut off all the available
meat, and, giving it a dust of salt and white
pepper, put it by. With all the bones, skin, and
any gravy that may be over, make the best game
broth possible. For this pound all the *enamelled*
bones before putting them into the pot, add any
trimmings of bacon or ham, a bunch of sweet
herbs, and an ounce of glaze ; cover with warm
water, boil, and simmer. When satisfied that
you have got all that the ingredients can yield,
strain the liquid off, and leave it in a bowl all
night. The next morning thicken this, add a
tablespoonful of Marsala, a teaspoonful of red-
currant jelly, one of anchovy vinegar, and such
seasoning as you may consider necessary. When
fully flavoured put in the meat, and let the *salmis*
warm slowly to steaming point without boiling,
keep in the *bain-marie* till required, and serve.
If the *whole* process were carried out overnight,
the dish would be all the better, gentle re-heating
being alone necessary the next day.

74. *Salmis of game.*

These may be either poached eggs on toast,

capped with "devil sauce" (No. 29, slightly thickened), or hard-boiled eggs cut in halves lengthwise, placed in a hot *entrée* dish, and moistened with "chutney sauce" (No. 8) as steaming hot as possible.

75. Deviled Eggs.

MENU XXVI.

Fried fish à l'Indienne.

Kubàb of liver and oysters.

Buttered eggs with shrimps.

Crumpets.

———

THIS depends upon a peculiar batter in which the fish is dipped before frying. Fillets of whiting may be chosen. Having prepared a bath of boiling fat, fry them, after having dipped them in this mixture :— *76. Fried fish à l'Indienne.*

Beat up two raw eggs in half a pint of milk, thicken this to the consistency of a batter that coats the spoon when lifted from it with *pea*-flour, add a saltspoonful of turmeric, a saltspoonful of ground ginger, and the same of salt and white pepper blended.

This is only a *kubàb* in so far that the viands are strung upon skewers in the Oriental manner. Choose about a pound of lamb's or calf's liver, and cut it into slices one-third of an inch thick, an inch wide, and an inch and a half long, egg *77. Kubâb* and crumb them with finely pounded *of liver* stale crumbs ; take one dozen cooking *and* oysters, and wrap each of them in *oysters.* a very thin slice of streaky bacon ; egg and bread these also with fine crumbs. Now pass these on to your skewers in alternate order—first a piece of liver, then an oyster, then a piece of liver, and so on ; melt a couple of ounces of clarified dripping in a frying-pan, and fry for three minutes on one side, then turn the skewers, and fry for three more on the other side ; drain, dry, and serve on a very hot dish.

A pint of picked shrimps, six eggs, and six toasts. Make buttered eggs of the eggs, butter *78. But-* the toasts, and toss the shrimps in a *tered eggs* frying-pan in a couple of ounces of *with* butter ; let them absorb the butter, *shrimps.* then turn them on to the toasts, and pour the hot buttered eggs over them.

MENU XXVII.

Fried shell-fish.

Chicken purée with mushrooms.

Egg molé.

Oatcakes.

A DISH of fried shell-fish, as is often presented at the Italian breakfast, is a nice variation from the ordinary routine. Take a dozen fair - sized shelled prawns, and a dozen shelled scallops ; make two pieces of *79.Fried shell-fish.* each prawn by slicing it lengthwise, and slice the scallops in the same way ; spread a layer of flour on a clean cloth, and roll the pieces of shell-fish in it ; let this dry, and then turn them, a ladleful at a time, into a bath of boiling fat. Fry a golden yellow, drain, and pile the crisp fritters (like whitebait) on a napkin ; dust salt over them, and serve with slices of lemon, brown bread-and-butter.

N.B. Scallops alone are quite acceptable when thus presented.

Enough minced chicken for the party should be made in the usual manner, and six mush-rooms, each the size of a five-shilling-piece, should be broiled or fried in butter. Butter six squares of fried bread, cover them with the steaming mince, and lay a fried mushroom on the top of each square.

80. *Chicken purée with mushrooms.*

Lay six poached or hard-boiled eggs in a hot silver *entrée* dish, and pour over them a sauce made like that given in No. 13, only use milk instead of fish broth for the moistening.

81. *Egg molé.*

MENU XXVIII.

ABSTINENCE.

Semolina fritters of fish.

Vegetable curry (Malay).

Eggs à la voyageuse.

Indian crumpets.

———

BOIL twelve ounces of semolina in sufficient milk
to form a paste. Let it get cold, then roll it out
a quarter of an inch thick, and line
a dozen oval tartlet moulds with it. *82. Semo-*
Fill these with a stiffly reduced *lina frit-*
ters of fish.
shrimp sauce, in which the shrimps,
cut into dice, are plentiful. Close over each
little patty thus formed with a covering of
semolina paste, wet the edges, pinch the tops
securely to the lining, and then take them out of
the moulds, egg, bread-crumb, and fry in very
hot fat, like *rissoles*. Drain, dry, and send in on
a napkin with fried parsley. These can be prepared, all but the frying, overnight. Remains of
lobster, oysters, scallops, or prawns, may be
similarly cooked.

7

Choose the following vegetables : Six cooked artichoke bottoms, the same weight of cooked vegetable marrow or cucumber, six sprigs of the flower of not over-cooked cauliflower, three cooked potatoes of moderate size. Cut the artichoke bottoms into four pieces each, cut the vegetable marrow also into pieces about the same size, and slice the potatoes into similarly small discs. Then proceed as explained for curried mushrooms (No. 20), serving rice with the curry as therein described.

83. Vegetable curry (Malay).

Lay six poached eggs on six fried toasts, and pour over each a little of this sauce : half a pint of milk thickened with a quarter of an ounce of butter, and the same of flour, flavoured with a tablespoonful of Harvey sauce, a dessertspoonful of tomato ketchup, a teaspoonful of anchovy vinegar, and salt to taste. A tablespoonful of milk with one raw yolk beaten up in it may be stirred in as a finishing touch, off the fire, just before using the sauce.

84. Eggs à la voyageuse.

MENU XXIX.

TRIM the hake into convenient pieces for frying, and *marinade* them as explained for the brill fillets (No. 73). Before cooking them, wipe the pieces carefully, make a good frying batter (No. 116) and prepare a bath of boiling fat. Dip the pieces into the batter, and fry them a rich golden brown. Serve piled upon a hot napkin.

85. *Orlys of fillets of hake.*

This simple dish can be made very tasty with a little trouble. Pass half a pound of lean Hamburg spiced or salt beef through the mincing machine ; cut the fat into dice, fry them till well melted, then empty the contents of the pan into a hot saucepan containing about a pint and a

86. *Twice-laid of salt beef.*

half of well-mashed potato : stir well together
with a wooden spoon, adding by degrees the
minced beef, and moistening the mixture with a
few spoonfuls of broth or milk. Turn the whole
into a well-buttered mould, and bake until
thoroughly hot, then turn out, and shake some
fine raspings over it. Garnish with curls of
bacon.

Bake overnight three good-sized onions on a
buttered dish until they are quite soft. Boil six
eggs hard. The next morning take off
87. Eggs
à la Bor-
delaise. the browned outer skin of the onions,
and mince them, and take four sardines
from the tin, free them from oil, and
cut them up rather small. Put an ounce of
butter into a frying-pan, throw into it the minced
onion, set the pan on a low fire, add the sardines,
fry very gently ; meanwhile warm the hard-boiled
eggs by putting them into hot water. All being
hot, empty the mince into a hot *entrée* dish, slice
the hard eggs, across, into pieces, strew them
over the mince, and serve very hot.

MENU XXX.

Kippered salmon.

Croquettes of mixed meat.

Omelettes with asparagus.

Muffins.

CUT six nice pieces from a kippered salmon, and, if necessary, soak them awhile to remove some of the saltness, then dry them, butter 88. *Kip-* them, and dust some pepper over them, *pered* then wrap in well-oiled papers, and broil *Salmon.* over the clearest fire on a gridiron.

These can be made of mixed cold meats over-night, and will be much improved by the remains of a *pâté de foie gras*, sweetbread, a 89. *Cro-* spoonful of ham or tongue if it can be *quettes of* spared, and the same of minced cooked *mixed* mushroom. But none of these ex- *meat.* pensive things is essential. Having minced the meat, seasoned, and flavoured it, stir it in a bowl in which you have poured a quarter of a pint of thick white or brown, sauce, with the yolks of

two raw eggs blended with it ; warm all in a
saucepan together, but without boiling, then put
aside the mixture to set firmly. Next morning
strew a pastry board with finely powdered and
sifted crumbs, divide the mince into equally
sized parts, roll them into drumlike shapes, egg,
crumb, and fry them in boiling fat till of a nice
yellow-brown colour ; drain, dry, and serve piled
up upon a hot napkin. Any nice brown sauce
can accompany.

Cooked asparagus, either fresh or tinned, may
be employed in this dish. Cut all the tender
part into quarter-inch dice, boil the
90. *Ome-* stalks in milk, strain, thicken the milk,
lette with season it with salt and pepper, and put
asparagus. the dice into it. Make two *omelettes*
as recommended in No. 6, and add the asparagus
as described in No. 24. Serve as hot as possible.

MENU XXXI.

FEW dishes of fish are nicer for breakfast than whitebait. They are none the worse for having been fried overnight ; on the contrary ; for a plunge into very hot fat for two, *91. White-bait.* or three minutes at most, and careful draining and drying, they are all the crisper. Serve them with slices of lemon and thin brown bread-and-butter in the usual way.

Vienna steaks are made in this way : Take half a pound of lean veal uncooked, and half a pound of lean beef also uncooked ; mince the two meats finely, season *92. Vienna steaks.* with spiced pepper and salt, and add a dessertspoonful of chopped parsley and a tea-spoonful of finely minced shallot ; mix into this two well-beaten eggs, and turn the whole out upon a flat dish. The mixture should be about three-eighths of an inch thick. This having been done the previous day, in the morning all that has to be done is to cut the now firm mass into rounds with a three and a half inch cutter; flour and fry them (*sauté*) in butter three minutes on one side, turn, and three minutes on the other, serving them on a hot dish in a circle, with a small mound of mashed potato in the centre. Plain brown gravy may accompany in a sauce boat.

The *omelettes* should be cooked in either of the ways already described (*see* No. 6, or 48), and the shrimps should be added in the manner 93. *Omelettes with shrimps.* explained for the mushrooms in No. 24. They should be prepared as follows: Having picked enough boiled shrimps to fill a half pint measure generously, pound the shells of the tails in a mortar with one ounce of butter, pass all through a hair-sieve, and put it into a small saucepan over a low fire, add the picked shrimps and a dust of mace, stir well to heat thoroughly, and spread half of the contents of the saucepan over the surface of each *omelette* just before turning the latter into the dish.

MENU XXXII.

Slices of Salmon, grilled.

Ham steaks.

Eggs in cases with mushrooms.

Irish scones.

CUT a piece of salmon into six slices half an inch thick. If the piece be a deep cut from the middle of a fine fish three slices will be sufficient, each being divided into two *94. Slices* pieces down the naturally marked divi- *of salmon,* sion of the fish. Remove the skin, and *grilled.* let the prepared slices lie all night in a *marinade* composed of four tablespoonfuls of salad oil, two of red wine vinegar, a dessertspoonful of chopped chives or finely shredded shallot, a tablespoonful of chopped parsley, and a sprinkling of spiced salt. In the morning lift the slices from the *marinade*, wipe them, and wrap them in well-buttered papers, twisting the ends of the papers to secure them firmly. Butter the bars of a well-cleaned gridiron, lay the cutlets one by one thereon, and boil them over a clear fire, turning them frequently. They will take about twelve minutes. If cut thicker, say three-quarters of an inch, and not wrapped in paper, they will be done in a quarter of an hour. In this case the slices must be buttered before being laid on the gridiron.

These are cut out of a raw ham in quarter-inch thick slices and broiled over a clear fire. The secret of success lies in having the ham, or a portion set aside for steaks, soaked as if for boiling, and to send the steaks in absolutely straight from the grill. Excellent steaks can thus be cut from a gammon of prime bacon, but the soaking and speedy service must be carried out with the same care.

95. *Ham steaks.*

Stew a quarter of a pound of trimmed mushrooms in milk ; when done, drain them, chop them up small with a silver dessert-knife. Thicken the milk custard-wise with the yolks of two raw eggs, stir in the minced mushroom and enough finely sifted white crumbs to bring the mixture to the consistency of a farce, seasoning with salt and a saltspoonful of spiced pepper. With this line half a dozen well-buttered china cases, leaving a hollow in the centre of each, into which break a fresh egg. Set the cases in a

96. *Eggs in cases with mush-rooms.*

shallow pan with hot water an inch deep round them, and poach them in the oven for eight or ten minutes. Pour enough of the sauce mentioned below to mask the top of each, dust over with fine raspings, and serve.

Sauce; only six dessertspoonfuls wanted. Take the trimmings of the mushrooms, wash, dry, and simmer them in just enough milk to cover them, for twenty minutes, season with a pinch each of salt and pepper; afterwards strain, thicken the broth thus obtained, and use as directed.

N.B.—The mushrooms should be prepared the day before.

MENU XXXIII.

Fish pudding with rice.

Grilled breast of mutton.

Eggs in coquilles.

Indian crumpets.

ANY cold fish carefully picked from the bones will do, or a combination of fish such as salmon and whiting, for a little salmon improves the pudding greatly. Take eight ounces of this, and four ounces of boiled rice, one hard-boiled egg crushed with a fork ; mix together in a bowl, seasoning with a saltspoonful of spiced pepper, and one of salt, and moistening with any fish sauce that may have been left, or milk, with one well-beaten egg. When worked to the consistency of a pudding, put the mixture into a buttered mould, place a round of paper over the exposed end, and set the mould in a large stewpan in boiling water one third of its depth ; cover the vessel, and let it steam for forty minutes (see p. 99). The mould

97. Fish pudding with rice.

can then be taken from the stewpan and the pudding turned out. If any fish broth be available, a white sauce, flavoured with a few drops of anchovy sauce, may be poured over the mould.

Trim and stew a breast of mutton or lamb with six ounces of onions, four ounces of carrot, an ounce of celery, a bouquet of herbs, and seasoning, with sufficient water to cover all well, till tender. Take the breast out of the broth, remove the bones at once, and place it between two dishes with a weight upon the upper one. This must be done while the meat is hot on the afternoon of the previous day. Save the broth. In the morning release the piece of meat from the weight, and cut it into neat pieces three inches long by one and a half wide. Score, and season these highly, grill, and serve with crisply fried parsley, and the "devil" sauce given for No. 29, using some of the broth that was saved in its making.

98. Grilled breast of mutton.

Boil six eggs hard. Fry a couple of fairly large mushrooms. Take the yolks out of the boiled eggs, chopping the whites into little squares, and treating the mushrooms in a similar manner. Mix the chopped whites and mushrooms, season

99. Eggs in co-quilles.

with spiced pepper and salt, and moisten them with a spoonful or two of good brown sauce ; add the crushed yolks with a little more sauce—just enough of the latter in all to form a nice moist mince.　Butter six china scallop shells, put an allowance of the mince in each, smoothing the surface in dome shape ; shake a layer of finely sifted white crumbs over them, pour a few drops of butter melted upon each, and set in the oven till nicely browned.　Serve very hot.

MENU XXXIV.

PUT a whole cod's roe, with the skin intact, into boiling water for five minutes. Take it out, put it on a sieve, and pour a jug of cold water over it. Then return it *100. Cod's-roe cutlets.* to the stewpan, to the water in which add a tablespoonful of vinegar and one of salt. Simmer slowly for twenty minutes, or thirty if a large roe. Then drain, and set it in the larder to get cold. When required in the morning, cut the roe into half-inch slices, trim these into cutlets with a cutter, egg, bread-crumb, and fry them a nice colour, then drain and dry, serving with brown bread-and-butter and sliced lemon.

These can be made out of any combination of cold meat, and if the following proportions be maintained—approximately—will be found very nice for breakfast : To two-thirds finely minced cold roast beef, mutton, veal, or fowl, allow one-third minced ham, tongue, mild lean bacon, or lean pressed beef. Blend a mince thus apportioned, season it with spiced pepper, and prepare half a pint of nicely flavoured brown gravy, slightly thickened. A good flavour will be got by adding to the gravy one tablespoon-ful mushroom ketchup, one dessertspoonful of Harvey sauce, a teaspoonful of vinegar from the walnut pickle, and a teaspoonful of Marsala. For seasoning a saltspoonful of sugar and one of salt. For the *croustades* choose six small stale dinner rolls ; slice off the rounded top of each as you take the top off a boiled egg ; then, using a fork, pick out the crumb without injuring the outer crust. Six bread-cases having thus been pre-pared, fry them in very hot beef dripping till pale golden in colour ; drain, dry, and keep till wanted. In the morning butter the inside of the cases, sprinkle over this a layer of finely minced parsley. Next, taking enough mince to fill each case, put it into a bowl, dilute with the sauce till nice and moist, fill the cases, strew a layer of fine crumbs over the tops, set them on a buttered baking tin, and put this into the oven for a few minutes, just till thoroughly hot. Meanwhile fry six curls of bacon, crisply, and

101. *Crou-stades of mixed meats.*

when serving the *croustades* put a curl on the top of each one.

In a small saucepan put a claret-glassful of tomato sauce, with a tablespoonful of melted glaze ; season with a saltspoonful of spiced pepper, dilute with broth or 102. *Eggs* milk to bring the liquid to the con- *on the dish* sistency of thin cream, then pass it *à la Mon-* through a strainer into a fire-proof *aco.* china dish ; break six eggs into this carefully without breaking, and put a few drops of melted butter. on each egg ; then set the dish in the oven, and as soon as the whites are set take it out, and serve on a napkin laid upon a larger dish.

MENU XXXV.

Haddock in a mould.

Chicken cutlets, Indian way.

Eggs on the dish with bacon.

Crumb-muffixs.

————————

TAKE the flesh from both sides of a medium-sized haddock. Put the head, skin, bones and tail, with an onion sliced, six pepper-

103. *Haddock in a mould.* corns, and a bouquet of herbs, into a stewpan with sufficient water to cover all ; season with a saltspoonful of salt, boil, and simmer for half an hour, then strain off the broth, which should be thickened with butter and flour (one ounce of each to half a pint), and finally enriched—off the fire—with the yolk of a raw egg. This being ready, proceed to pound the flesh of the haddock in a mortar, moistening it during the operation with a spoonful or two of the sauce. When well pounded pass the fish through the sieve, and to it add half its bulk of white bread-crumb that has been soaked in milk ;

pound all together, moisten slightly with the
sauce and two well-beaten eggs, seasoning with
spiced pepper. When well mixed, butter a plain
pudding mould, fill it with the mixture, and
poach it " *au-bain marie* "—*i.e.*, place it one-third
deep in boiling water, watch it come again to the
boil, then lower the fire and steam as you would
a pudding, closely covered, for three-quarters of
an hour. In the morning set the mould again in
hot water, and keep it so until thoroughly heated
through, when it should be turned out upon a
hot dish. Any unexpended sauce there may be
should be warmed and poured over the mould.

The legs and thighs of fowls, the breasts of
which have been used for an *entrée*, will do well.
The meat may be cooked or not. The
remains of a turkey may be thus 104. *Chic-*
utilised. To three-quarters of a pound *ken cutlets,*
of cold cooked meat allow six ounces *Indian*
of cold cooked pork sausage. Mince *way.*
the meat, not too finely, and chop up the
sausages, removing the skin ; add a teaspoonful
of minced shallot, a dessertspoonful of parsley,
and a sprinkling of salt ; mix all together with
two raw eggs, spread the mixture on a dish three-
eighths of an inch thick, and let it stiffen during
the night. In the morning cut it into cutlets
with a cutter, flour them, and lay them in a
sauté pan with an ounce of butter. Fry six

minutes (three on each side), and dish in a circle with fried parsley as garnish.

Cut into thin slices enough cold cooked bacon to cover the bottom of a large fire-proof dish.
105. *Eggs on the dish with bacon.* Slightly butter the dish, cut the slices into inch squares, and lay them over the bottom of the dish. Put it into the oven, let the bacon cook for five minutes on one side, then turn the pieces and cook five minutes longer. Now take the dish out of the oven and break six eggs into it, return it to the oven till the whites are set, then dish in the manner described for No. 102.

MENU XXXVI.

ABSTINENCE.

Sole as whitebait.

Mushroom fritters.

Omelette à la Soubise.

Barley-meal scones.

———

THIS is a fanciful way of serving fried sole, which, as a change, may be acceptable. Skin a medium-sized fish, and detach the long fillets on either side of the spine. Cut *106. Sole* these into strips about the size of a *as white-bait.* largish whitebait, toss them in a floured cloth, and plunge them in relays into a bath of boiling lard or clarified suet, in which a frying-basket has been set ; in six or seven minutes they should just turn colour, when lift the basket out of the bath, drain for a moment over the pan, then turn out upon a sheet of blotting-paper placed in front of the fire so as to dry. When all have thus been fried, drained, and dried, sprinkle them with salt, dish on a very hot dish, serving with brown bread-and-butter and lemon cut into quarters.

Half a pound of good fresh mushrooms should be chosen. It is never advisable to buy these very nice fungi after they have turned black. Commence by boiling two eggs hard ; while this is proceeding, trim, peel, and prepare the mushrooms, putting all the stalks and peelings into a saucepan, with a pinch of mignonette pepper and two of salt ; cover with milk, milk and water, or water, according to your resources, and bring once to the boil, simmering afterwards for twenty minutes ; then strain through muslin — for there may be grit in the mushroom trimmings —and save the broth in a bowl. Thicken this with a quarter of an ounce of butter and a quarter of an ounce of flour, reducing it somewhat, and lastly add (off the fire) the yolk of a raw egg. Next cut the mushrooms up into a coarse mince, and, putting this into a *sauté* pan with an ounce of butter, fry it for five minutes over a moderate fire. Remove the pan from the fire. Chop up the hard-boiled eggs, whites and yolks together, and add this to the fried minced mushroom, seasoning with a teaspoonful of spiced pepper and salt. Dilute this with a few spoonfuls of the sauce, and again, over a moderate fire, proceed to cook the mixture, adding a little more sauce if it seems necessary. When the mixture thickens well, stop, turn the contents of the pan out upon a dish, pat it into

107.*Mushroom fritters.*

shape with a wooden spoon, making it about a quarter of an inch thick, and leave it to get firm during the night. In the morning cut this into cutlets ; egg, bread-crumb, and fry a golden brown, and serve with fried parsley.

In this case an onion *purée à la Soubise* is added to an *omelette* just as the latter is on the point of being passed into the dish. Cook the *omelettes* (for there had better be two, as already advised) in either of the two methods (No. 6 or 48) that 108. *Omelette à la Soubise.* have been given, adding, at the period indicated, this *purée*, which would of course be made overnight.

Mince six ounces of onion, plunge this into boiling water to blanch for seven or eight minutes ; strain carefully, turn the mince into a stewpan, and over a low fire ; stir it about to dry thoroughly, then add a tablespoonful of milk, simmer, and continue adding by degrees till the onion is covered with milk ; now simmer till the onion is cooked, then strain, pass the mince through the sieve, thicken the milk in which it was boiled with a quarter of an ounce of butter and the same of flour, pass in the *purée*, amalgamate thoroughly, adding the yolk of an egg beaten up in a tablespoonful of milk to finish with.

MENU XXXVII.

Sea-bream on the dish.

Chicken à la chevalier.

Buttered eggs with mushrooms.

Brown rolls.

FILLET a sea-bream neatly. With all the trimmings make a broth as described in No. 103 ;
when this is ready strain it into a shallow

109. Sea-bream on the dish. pan just large enough to hold the fillets ; a copper *sauté* pan with an upright rim will do ; place this on the fire,
bring to the boil, put in the fillets, and in three minutes reduce the heat to simmering ; in eight or ten minutes the fillets will be sufficiently done for our purpose. Put them aside for the night, carefully saving the broth. In the morning thicken the broth, giving it a teaspoonful of anchovy sauce, and having arranged the fillets on a buttered flat dish that will stand the oven pour the sauce over them in sufficient quantity to mask them neatly ; dust over the surface a layer

of finely grated cheese, and set the dish in the oven just long enough to heat thoroughly ; remove it when this has taken place, pass a heated glazing iron over the surface to make it a yellowish brown, and serve. Any cold cooked fish may be similarly dressed. Serve of course on the dish in which it was cooked.

An easy way of presenting a *réchauffé* of chicken, fowl, or turkey. Remove the legs and thighs from a pair of cold roast or boiled birds, put them aside while you pick 110. *Chicken à la chevalier.* off all the remaining meat on the carcases. Pick all the burnt skin out of this, and chop up the bones that remain, with which proceed to make a broth. Pass the meat through the mincing machine or chop it upon a board. Season this with spiced pepper and salt. Thicken the broth slightly, and moisten the mince with it, heating the mixture in the *bain-marie*. Score, season, and grill the joints that were cut off in the first instance, dishing as follows : On the bottom of a hot silver dish place a piece of crisply fried bread for each piece of grilled fowl, spread a layer of the mince on each of these, and place the leg or thigh over that, garnishing the whole with crisply fried curls of bacon. In the case of a turkey the joints must be cut crosswise into convenient pieces.

Buttered eggs with mushrooms can either be served upon toasts—first the mushrooms and then a covering of the egg mixture— *111. Buttered eggs with mushrooms.* or a layer of mushrooms can be laid on the bottom of a hot silver dish with the buttered eggs over them. A third way is to incorporate the mushrooms with the buttered eggs the last thing before dishing the latter. Prepare the eggs as shown in No. 3, and the mushrooms as in No. 36.

MENU XXXVIII.

Cutlets of moulded fish.

Ox-tongue fillets devilled.

Eggs in cases with ham.

Crumpets.

PREPARE on the day before the cutlets are wanted a mould of fish as explained in the case of "haddock mould" (No. 103). This can be made of mixed fish, and if any salmon, remains of lobster, or shrimps can be worked in with it, so much the better. Put the mould away at night, and in the morning cut it into neat pieces—cutlet shapes if liked—which egg, bread-crumb, fry in boiling fat a golden brown, and serve crisp and dry with fried parsley.

112. Cutlets of moulded fish.

Cut from a cold boiled tongue eight or ten neat slices a quarter of an inch thick ; prepare as

many rounds of fried bread ; get ready half
113. *Ox-* a pint of the "devil sauce" already
tongue explained in No. 29. Trim the tongue
fillets slices free from skin, and season them
devilled. with grill seasoning (No. 29). Give
them a few turns on the gridiron, lay them on
the toasts, and pour the sauce over them.

Butter six china cases or scallop shells ; take
enough finely grated ham to fill an afternoon tea-
cup ; moisten this with twice the quan-
114. *Eggs* tity of good brown sauce and stir in
in cases the yolk of a raw egg off the fire when
with ham. the mixture is ready. With this line
your cases or shells, leaving a hollow space in
the middle of each to hold an egg. Put the
cases in hot water to poach and set the lining,
then take them out. In the morning warm
the cases, slip a poached egg into the hollow
of each of them, pour a dessertspoonful of hot
brown sauce over every egg, and serve.

MENU XXXIX.

Baked smelts.

Kromeskis of chicken.

Eggs with oysters.

Devilled biscuits.

———————

LARGE smelts are the best for this dish. Butter an oval fire-proof dish, sprinkle finely minced parsley over it, on this bed lay one dozen smelts ; moisten them with half a pint *115. Baked smelts.* of white sauce, strew them over with fine raspings pretty thickly, put into a moderate oven for ten minutes, and serve in their dish placed on a napkin.

Make a mixture of chicken—or veal with ham, lean bacon, or any tasty adjunct—as if for *croquettes* (No. 89). In the morning mix a frying batter : Put four and a *116. Kro-meskis of chicken.* half ounces of flour into a bowl, make a hollow in the centre and put into it a quarter of a pint of water, half a saltspoonful of

salt, the yolks of two eggs, and two tablespoonfuls of salad oil. Mix thoroughly till the batter
coats the spoon with a coating the eighth of an
inch thick, adding water, if necessary, to attain
that consistency. Twenty minutes before using
stir in the whites of the two eggs well whipped.
For the kromeskis cut out of thinly sliced cooked
bacon eight or a dozen pieces about three inches
long and two inches wide ; lay a tablespoonful
of the minced meat in the centre of each of these,
roll them up, dip them into the batter, and fry in
a bath of boiling fat till they turn a light brown
colour ; drain, dry, and serve on a napkin.

The oysters should be prepared the previous
evening. The operation is very simple, yet it
requires care. Order a dozen sauce
117. *Eggs* oysters to be sent up *with their liquor*.
with oy- Strain the latter, for it is often gritty
sters. with little atoms of shell, into a small
saucepan, putting in with it the beards taken
from the oysters ; add fish broth, milk or water
to moisten well, and boil, simmering afterwards
for half an hour. Strain off this liquid, let it get
cold, put the bearded oysters into it, empty it all
into a saucepan and set it on the fire—the heat
moderate—watch now, and the moment *signs* of
boiling can be detected, stop ; reduce the heat to
the *lowest* simmering temperature, and in two
minutes the oysters will be ready. If allowed to

boil the oysters will be leathery. Now take out the oysters, thicken the broth, put them in again, and keep this in a china or earthenware bowl during the night.

In the morning boil six eggs hard ; cool them in cold water ; slice them crosswise, butter a fire-proof baking dish, put a layer of the eggs at the bottom of it, arrange the oysters, now taken out of the sauce, over this, and cover with another layer of egg slices, seasoning each layer with pepper and salt, moisten the whole with the oyster sauce, cover the surface with raspings somewhat thickly strewn, and put the dish in the oven until steaming, when serve. This is obviously an easy way of disposing of any oyster sauce left from dinner the previous evening.

MENU XL.

GET the whiting untouched by the fishmonger except cleaning. Put the fish (three or four, according to size) upon a dish over-

118. Scalded whitings. night, squeeze a lemon over them, and sprinkle with salt. In the morning put a fish-kettle with drainer on the fire with as much water as you think will cover the fish nicely, add to it a dessertspoonful of vinegar and a teaspoonful of salt, wipe each fish, and when the water boils put them into the kettle ; this will stop the boiling ; let it come up to the boil again, then draw back the vessel ; from five to eight minutes must now be allowed, according to size ; drain as soon as tender, getting rid of all the water from the fish, and serve with slices of lemon and brown bread-and-butter. This is perhaps

the most easily digested dish of fish that can be
presented either at breakfast or any other meal.
It is equally practicable with small-sized fresh
haddock.

Take two pounds of potatoes (weighed after
paring), steam or boil, pass through the sieve,
moisten in a bowl with two well-beaten
eggs, work to the consistency of smooth   119. *Potato
dough, adding a spoonful of milk if   cutlets.*
necessary.   Spread a slight layer of flour on a
board, turn the potato dough upon it, flour and
roll it out as you would ordinary dough for
pastry.   Sift a thin layer of finely grated cheese
over the surface, and dust over with salt and
spiced pepper ; fold over, roll out again, fold, and
put it away.   Prepare eight or ten tablespoonfuls
of any nice minced meat, moistening it as explained for *croquettes* (No. 89).   Set this aside
also.   In the morning roll out the potato paste a
quarter of an inch thick with a three-inch cutter,
cut this into rounds, put a tablespoonful of the
croquette mixture on each round, fold over, and
pinch the edges securely.   Brush over with egg,
roll in finely sifted crumbs, and either heat them
up on a buttered baking tin in the oven, or
plunge till well coloured in boiling fat.

Choose six scallop shells ; put into them a
lining of roughly minced kidney prepared in

this way :—Take a pair of fine mutton kidneys, or half a veal kidney, previously cooked—those taken out of a cold roast joint will do ; cut them up into small squares, moisten the mince with a quarter of a pint of any brown sauce there may be left, or thickened gravy from a joint, flavoured with a tablespoonful of mushroom ketchup. Heat up this in the morning and use as follows : —Having lined each shell with the mince, slip a poached egg into the hollow, put a teaspoonful of the sauce on each egg, and serve.

120. Poached eggs à la Colbert.

MENU XLI.

Herring fillets fried.

Rabbit au gratin.

Eggs with artichokes.

Tea-cake—not sweetened.

———

TAKE the flesh from four fresh herrings, one
long fillet from each side. Save the roes. Put
the fillets overnight on a flat dish,
sprinkle them with salt, and squeeze 121. *Her-*
a few drops of lemon juice over each of *ring fil-*
them. Give the roes a fry and put *lets fried.*
them away—they will come in for " a savoury "
at dinner the next day. In the morning wipe,
egg, bread-crumb, and fry the fillets as crisply as
possible in boiling fat, serving them nicely dried
after draining on a napkin, slices of lemon
accompanying.

Pick all the meat remaining from a couple of
boiled rabbits, the back fillets of which may have
been used at a previous meal ; save all the onion

sauce that may have been left, and as much of
the boilings as may not have been used. Butter
a fire-proof baking dish, strew this over with
finely minced parsley, arrange the pieces
122. Rab- of meat over this, dusting them with
bit au spiced pepper and salt, and moistening
gratin. with the onion sauce supplemented
with a spoonful or two of the boilings thickened.
Having finished the packing, dredge a good
layer of raspings over the surface of the
rabbit, and put the dish into a moderate oven to
heat thoroughly. If well moistened, this will be
found a nice dish for a change.

This should be made with artichoke bottoms
(*fonds d'artichauts*), but a decidedly nice combination can be made with Jerusalem arti-
123. *Eggs* chokes. Arrange six cooked artichoke
with arti- bottoms on a buttered fire-proof dish,
chokes. pour a few drops of melted butter on
each, warm in the oven, take out the dish, put a
nicely trimmed poached egg upon each, sprinkle
a dust of spiced pepper over each, or a drop or
two of tarragon vinegar, and serve. When made
with Jerusalem artichokes, the *purée* is the
simplest method to choose for the vegetable ;
line a well-buttered fire-proof dish with this,
dust a fine layer of grated cheese over the surface, dress the poached eggs neatly in hollows
scooped out of this bed, and serve.

———

PRACTICABLE with small trout.   Clean six quarter-
pounders, trim, sprinkle them with salt, and fry
them in butter in the *sauté* pan.   Put
them, when thus cooked, in a deep dish, 124. *Trout*
and let them get cold, pouring over *fried and*
them a marinade composed of four *marinadea.*
tablespoonfuls of salad oil and three of anchovy
vinegar, seasoned with a teaspoonful of finely
grated horseradish, a tablespoonful of chopped
parsley, a teaspoonful of chopped thyme or
marjoram, and one of chives if not objected to.
Let this stand all night, and serve as it is.   An
excellent summer dish.

Prepare the vermicelli exactly as explained for
spaghetti (No. 62), cutting it up small and adding

a coffeecupful of tomato conserve to it, a quarter of a pint of white sauce, and two raw eggs. Stir altogether over a low fire, then spread the mixture upon a dish during the night for it to stiffen. In the morning shape this into little ovals as described for meat *croquettes* (No 89), and cook in the same manner. If liked, the ovals may be rolled in crushed uncooked vermicelli instead of bread crumbs.

125. *Croquettes of vermicelli.*

Pound in a mortar two ounces of carefully picked and scalded leaves of chervil, parsley, chives, tarragon, and watercress with six capers and the fillet of a boned anchovy ; pass the whole through the sieve, and stir it into half a pint of white sauce. Arrange six poached eggs on fried squares of bread and pour a portion of the sauce over each.

126. *Eggs with green herb sauce.*

MENU XLIII.

———————

FOR these turn to No. 117, and follow the directions therein given both in regard to the making of the oyster broth, and the cooking of the oysters, but using **127. *Oyster cutlets.*** eighteen sauce oysters instead of twelve. After the latter have been cooked drain them from the broth, and put them on a plate. Next, presuming there is about half a pint of broth, proceed with half an ounce of butter and half an ounce of flour to thicken it ; while cooling somewhat, cut the oysters up into small pieces and put them with two ounces of bread-crumb soaked in milk and the yolks of two raw eggs into the broth, stir together over a low fire to thicken, but do not boil on any account, and then turn the mixture out on a dish, and leave it in a cool

larder for the night. In the morning shape the
mixture in flat oval shapes with two wooden
spoons, or cut them with a cutlet cutter, egg,
bread-crumb, and fry in boiling fat ; drain, dry,
and serve with slices of lemon and brown bread-
and-butter.

This homely dish can be made worthy of service
at any table if a little trouble be taken with the
potato, the dishing up, and the frying
of the sausages. Taking the last first,
128. *Sausages with potatoes.* to preserve the sausages in shape without bursting, *time* must be taken—that
is to say, the sausages, having been pricked, must
be put in melted beef dripping over a *low* fire
and cooked slowly and thoroughly. People who
think that sausages are too rich will find them
much plainer if they be partly boiled before
frying. Prick them well, put them into hot
water, bring slowly to the boil for fear of bursting,
then simmer for five minutes ; after this they can
be drained and fried till brown. For the potato :
Boil or steam half a dozen fairly sized potatoes,
drain, mash, pass through the sieve, moisten with
an ounce of butter and a coffeecupful of milk,
season with a teaspoonful of spiced pepper and a
dessertspoonful of grated cheese, add the yolk of
a raw egg, mix thoroughly, pat into six neat,
elongated ovals, set these on a buttered baking
tin, which put in the oven till thoroughly hot ;

take the tin from the oven, with a slice lift the
potato ovals, lay them on a hot dish, put a well-
drained sausage, free from all fat, upon each, and
serve.

Cut up six tomatoes weighing in all, say, three-
quarters of a pound ; cut up very finely one
small shallot, say, half an ounce. Put
half an ounce of butter at the bottom   129. *Eggs
of a small stewpan, melt it and put   *à la Portu-
in the minced shallot, season with   *gaise.*
spiced pepper and salt, fry over a low fire till
turning pale golden brown, then add the tomatoes, increase the fire, now stirring the tomatoes
well, the object being to reduce their wateriness
somewhat. When nicely pulped, pass the mixture through the sieve and put it aside. In the
morning butter a fire-proof china dish, arrange
the *purée* on the bottom of it, warm this in the
oven, take it out, hollow out with a spoon six
little cavities in the tomato bed and slip a raw
fresh egg into each of them. Place the dish in
the oven again till the eggs have set nicely, and
serve.

MENU XLIV.

Fillets of brill à la meunière.

Devilled sheep's tongues.

Fried eggs and bacon.

Oatmeal scones.

————————

HAVING procured eight or ten nice fillets of brill, lay them on a flat dish,. lightly sprinkle them with salt, and squeeze a few drops of lemon juice over them. In the morning wipe them, flour them, and having melted a couple of ounces of butter in a *sauté* pan over a low fire, put them therein, turning them frequently till done ; then drain and arrange them on a hot dish ; add another ounce of butter (melted) to the butter in the *sauté* pan, let this turn a pale brown ; then take the pan from the fire, add a teaspoonful of anchovy sauce to the butter, let it froth, and stir in little by little a couple of tablespoonfuls of vinegar that has been warmed separately, and a teaspoonful of finely-minced parsley. Empty

130. Fillets of brill à la meunière.

this over the fried fillets, and serve. The point of this method of cooking fish will be entirely lost unless the dish containing the fillets be as hot as possible, and the sauce that is added equally so. It must be served without any delay whatever.

The six sheep's tongues must be cooked until tender, and skinned on the previous day. In the morning trim off the unsightly roots of the tongues, dip them in melted butter, lay them on a buttered gridiron, and let them just catch the fire nicely. Arrange them upon a hot dish on *croûtons* of fried bread with a crisp curl of bacon between each, and a masking over them of the sauce given for No. 29, the basis of which can be the broth in which the tongues were cooked.

131. Devil-led sheep's tongues.

One of the very commonest of breakfast dishes in the British Isles is fried eggs and bacon. In the majority of cases it may be described as an arrangement of eggs in a condition of boot-leather, surrounded by greasy slices of bacon, and resting upon a layer of discoloured melted fat. Now it is by no means easy to fry an egg properly. The usual way in vogue is to put the eggs, three or four at once, into the far too scanty quantity of melted fat in which the bacon was cooked. This

132. Fried eggs and bacon.

method is altogether wrong. In the first place, the eggs and the bacon must be prepared separately, the former being fried one by one as follows : Empty four ounces of fresh lard into a small but deep frying-pan, just large enough to hold the fat when melted and accommodate one egg. Heat the lard as for whitebait, and when ready, slope the frying-pan so that you can slide gently upon its surface a fresh egg, previously broken from the shell into a large spoon. It will set very quickly, lift with a perforated slice, drain thoroughly, and proceed with the next. Six eggs having thus been fried, dried, and trimmed as to their edges, lay them on squares of fried bread upon a hot dish, garnishing with curls of crisply-fried bacon, or with bacon cut into small squares and similarly *dry*-fried.

MENU XLV.

Fried sprats.

Broiled fowl with mushrooms.

Eggs with liver.

Irish scones.

————

WHEN sprats are in season they make a nice breakfast dish. Treat them as much as possible as you would whitebait : flour, fry at a gallop in a boiling fat, drain, dry well, sprinkle with salt, and serve with brown bread-and-butter and lemon. They may be egged, crumbed, and served as smelts, but this is more troublesome than flouring. *133. Fried sprats.*

Choose the drumsticks and thighs of a couple of cold roast fowls ; score, rub with butter, season with salt and spiced pepper, and grill on a well-buttered gridiron. Treat six or eight nice-sized mushrooms in mush-like manner. Dish the latter on croûtons of fried bread with the broiled fowl arranged round them. *134. Broiled fowl with mushrooms.*

If there happen to be any fowl, turkey, or rabbit livers available, or three ounces of lamb's

135. *Eggs with liver.*　or veal liver, cooked, cut it up into small squares, which keep ready on a plate, dusting them over with salt and spiced pepper. Put into a small saucepan half an ounce of butter with half an ounce of finely-minced shallot, fry till turning colour over a low fire, then add half an ounce of flour, mix and continue the frying for five minutes, then stir in half a pint of broth, meat gravy, or soup that may have been left, let the sauce come to the boil, then simmer, adding one tablespoonful of mushroom ketchup, a teaspoonful of walnut-pickle vinegar, and half one of red-currant jelly. Mix well and pass through a strainer into a clean bowl, empty the mince into this, and set it aside for the night. In the morning warm the liver sauce in the *bain-marie*, adding a dessert-spoonful of marsala. Keep this hot while you prepare a fire-proof china dish, then put in the liver, making little hollows for the reception of six fresh eggs. These having been put in, set the dish in the oven till the eggs are set, and serve.

MENU XLVI.

Salmon fritters.

Veal and ham scallops.

Buttered eggs with fines herbes.

Indian-meal rolls.

THESE can be made out of the remains of cold salmon in this manner : Cut up the salmon in small pieces, take an equal quantity of breadcrumb—say six ounces of each— *136. Salmon* empty both into a bowl, season plainly *fritters.* with pepper and salt, moisten with any sauce that has been left, or with a quarter of a pint of white sauce made with the salmon boilings. Add two raw yolks, mix thoroughly, and spread the mixture upon a flat dish, a quarter of an inch thick, cover, and leave for the night. In the morning cut with a two and a half inch cutter a series of rounds out of the flattened mixture, flour them, or dip them in frying batter (No. 116), plunge them into boiling fat till golden-brown ; drain, dry, and serve with sliced lemon.

Having prepared a mince of cold veal and ham—two-thirds of the former to one of the latter—season it with salt and spiced pepper, and moisten it with a white sauce made out of veal broth. Butter six or eight fire-proof china scallop-shells, or a large baking-dish, sprinkle over the butter a coating of finely-minced cooked mushroom, put in the minced meat, dust over the surface of the scallops with fine raspings, pour a few drops of butter, melted, over them, and warm in the oven, serving with a curl of fried bacon on each.

137. Veal and ham scallops

This is a variation ot buttered eggs. *Fines herbes* is to be described as a mixture of mushrooms, parsley and shallot, or chives if procurable, in these proportions—equal measure of the two former to one-third of the last. For this dish a tablespoonful of chopped mushroom (well cleaned fresh trimmings will do) and one of chopped parsley to a dessertspoonful or rather less of chopped shallot. Begin by frying the shallot in a quarter of an ounce of butter, a pinch of pepper and one of salt, over a low fire for five minutes, then stir in the parsley and mushroom, fry for five minutes more. Empty the contents of the pan into a bowl and set aside. In the morning put a quarter of an ounce of butter into

138. Buttered eggs with fines herbes.

a small saucepan, add a quarter of an ounce of
flour, cook over a low fire for four or five minutes,
then stir in a quarter of a pint of milk, bring to
the boil to thicken, simmer, adding the *fines
herbes* and a dessertspoonful of milk, with which
a raw yolk has been beaten, keeping it hot afterwards in the *bain-marie*. Now make the buttered
eggs (No. 3), adding the *fines herbes* mixture as a
finishing touch. Serve as hot as possible.

MENU XLVII.

Cod in custard sauce.

Dry curry on toast.

Matelote of eggs.

Vienna rolls.

———————

TAKE a pound and a quarter of cold boiled cod-fish and break it up into nice flaky pieces. Put these into a stewpan, season with pepper, salt, and a grate of nutmeg, and moisten with enough of the boilings, saved the previous evening, to cover ; set this in the *bain-marie* to heat up slowly, while with the yolks of a couple of eggs you proceed to turn half a pint of the boilings to a savoury custard, when ready drain the now hot pieces of fish from the liquid in which they were warmed, arrange them on a hot dish, and smother with the custard. Serve as hot as possible.

139. *Cod in custard sauce.*

This is a very nice breakfast "savoury." Make on the day previous a good curry of one pound

of mutton, veal, or lamb cut into neat squares,
and put it away for the night in a china dish.
In the morning prepare eight or ten two
and a half inch squares of fried bread, 140. *Dry
and lay these in close order in a hot curry on toast.*
silver dish. Pick the pieces of meat out
of the curry gravy, and melt half an ounce of
butter in a stewpan or earthenware casserole, set
this over a very low fire, put in the curried meat,
stirring it about so as to heat up and dry at the
same time. The process must be patiently
carried out, and care must be taken to prevent
burning. When quite hot the dry curry should
be arranged on the fried bread, and served with
curls of crisply fried bacon or fried ham. If
preferred the curry may be simply warmed,
without drying, in the *bain-marie*, and poured
over the toasts. This, it need scarcely be said, is
a handy way of serving the remains of a curry
left at a previous meal.

Put an ounce of butter at the bottom of a stewpan over a low fire, melt it, add an ounce of flour,
slowly cook these together for seven
minutes till browning lightly, then add 141. *Matelote of eggs.*
a pint of broth, gravy, or clear soup
that may have been left, flavour with a tablespoonful of mushroom ketchup, a saltspoonful of
spiced pepper, salt if necessary, and a sherry-
glass of light claret ; boil, skim, and pass this

sauce into a fire-proof dish, then slip six eggs into it, put the dish in the oven and poach them till set, when serve.

N.B.—When red wine is used in cookery the vessel should either be enamelled or glazed earthenware : tinned utensils have a prejudicial effect on the colour of the sauce in these circumstances.

MENU XLVIII.

Water-zootje.

Fritot of pigeons.

Eggs with tarragon.

Devilled biscuits.

IF this dish has been presented on the previous evening it can be easily heated for breakfast, for which meal, owing to its plainness, it is very well suited. A zootje can be made of any fish, or any mixture of fish, including the fresh water varieties. The flounder is a favourite subject for treatment in this fashion, but whiting, small haddock, slips, &c., are very nice in a zootje. The first thing to do is to fillet the fish and make a good broth with the heads, bones, and trimmings, using the adjuncts mentioned in No. 103, and when nicely flavoured to strain it off and employ it as the "water" in which the fillets are to be cooked. Bring the "water" to the boil, put in the fillets, let it return to the boil for a minute, then simmer

142. Water zootje.

the fillets till done ; bunches of green parsley
should be boiled with a zootje, the scraped root
of parsley also, and a tablespoonful of grated
horseradish is an improvement if there be as
much as three pints of water or broth. Serve
the fillets in a deep dish with the parsley and the
broth as well, brown bread-and-butter accompanying. In hot weather a nice breakfast dish is *cold*
zootje, for if the decoction of the heads and
bones be strong, and the dish be set in a very
cold larder or upon a bed of crushed ice, it will
solidify in a firm jelly. A little gelatine may be
added.

Three pigeons will be enough if of a good size.
Slightly roast and split them in halves. Marinade
these during the night with three table-
143. *Fritot*   spoonfuls of salad oil, the juice of a
of pigeons.   lemon, a bunch of parsley shredded, a
half ounce shallot also sliced finely, a dozen pepper
corns, and a dust of salt. In the morning take
out of the marinade and wipe the pieces of
pigeon, dip them in milk, flour them well,
plunge them in very hot fat (as for *croquettes*)
when they turn a pale brown, drain, dry, dish on
a napkin or paper, garnish with fried parsley, and
serve. Should there be any bread sauce available
it would be an appropriate adjunct. By saving
the livers of the birds you can dish them effect-
ively in this manner. Fry the livers in butter,

empty them and the butter into a mortar, pound
them, add for six livers a teaspoonful of anchovy
essence, season with a saltspoonful of spiced
pepper, and spread the mixture on six nicely
fried toasts, heat in the mouth of the oven, and
lay a half pigeon on each, serving immediately.

This may be done with either poached or hard-
boiled eggs. If the former, put an ounce of
butter in a small saucepan, take it off the
fire when half melted, so that it may 144. *Eggs*
complete the melting in the hot sauce- *with*
pan, add a teaspoonful of lemon juice *tarragon.*
and the same of chopped tarragon, or, if tarragon
be out of season, a teaspoonful of tarragon
vinegar instead of lemon juice ; a teaspoonful of
this should be poured over each of the six poached
eggs after the latter have been arranged on
squares of buttered toast. For hard-boiled
eggs : Slice them in halves, longitudinally, and
lay them in a hot silver dish, masking them with
white sauce flavoured with chopped tarragon.

PREPARE one large or two medium-sized soles as if for frying, No. 28, but in this instance the

145. *Soles in the oven.* fish can be left whole. Butter a flat *gratin* dish, sprinkle this over with finely chopped parsley, lay the sole upon it and moisten the upper side of the fish with butter, melted. Put this in the oven; after eight minutes' cooking carefully turn the sole, baste again with butter, and six minutes afterwards it will be done. Lift the fish with a slice and put it upon the hot dish prepared for it; to the butter in the *gratin* dish add a tablespoonful of minced parsley and the juice of a lemon: pour this over the dished sole and serve immediately. As in all cases where butter melted forms the sauce of a dish of

fish great care must be taken to have things as hot as possible, to prevent greasiness.

For these follow the directions given for No. 107, but with this difference as to proportions : Four hard-boiled eggs instead of two, and a quarter of a pound of mushrooms instead 146. *Egg croquettes.* of double that quantity. Mix the two minces as therein explained, adding one filleted anchovy, minced small, or a teaspoonful of the essence. When thickened pat the mixture into shape in the same way, but making it about two-thirds of an inch thick. In the morning divide the mass into pieces, which when rolled in fine crumbs will be about the size of a guinea-fowl's egg. Brush over with beaten egg and crumb these, plunging them one by one into very hot fat ; as soon as they turn a nice golden colour take them out, drain, dry, dust over with salt, and serve piled up on a napkin or paper.

See No. 117. In this instance, before being finally added to the thickened broth, each oyster should be cut into two pieces. Divide the mixture in halves—one for each 147. *Omelettes with oysters.* *omelette* (which can be made in either of the ways given—No. 6 or 48, as may be preferred), and having heated it in the *bain-marie* pass one portion into each *omelette* as done in the case of No. 93.

MENU L.

Fillets of brill with tomatoes.

Jambalaia of fowl.

Omelettes with salmon.

Sally lunns.

———————

FOR this please turn to No. 109, and treat a nice-sized brill exactly in the manner described for
148. Fillets of brill with tomatoes. the sea bream. Proceed in all respects similarly until the thickening of the broth stage, when the teaspoonful of anchovy sauce should be omitted, and two tablespoonfuls of tomato conserve added instead. This, when nice and smooth, should be poured over the fish fillets as explained in the before-mentioned recipe ; the glazing is, however, unnecessary.

A "*jambalaia*" is a species of European khitchri ; that is to say, it consists of minced chicken and ham tossed in rice, the process being thus conducted : Boil six ounces of rice as for curry (No. 20) ; chop up five ounces of uncooked lean ham, and eight or ten ounces of cold cooked chicken. Put the ham into a small frying-pan with an ounce of butter and give it a fry till fit to serve, then stir in the cooked chicken, season with spiced 149. *Jam-balaia of fowl.* pepper, and turn the contents of the pan into the vessel containing the hot rice, which by this time should be drained and dry. Serve well mixed on a very hot dish.[1]

Here the method is as nearly as possible the same as that adopted for the oyster *omelette*, and by its means half a pound of cold cooked salmon can be turned to capital account. Break up the salmon, but not too finely, and moisten it in a stewpan over a low 150. *Omelettes with salmon.* fire, or in the *bain-marie*, either with the sauce left the previous evening or a quarter of a pint of melted butter sauce made with the salmon boilings. Add half of this, quite hot, but not boiling, to each of the *omelettes* in the same way as the oysters in No. 147.

[1] This dish is improved by stirring into the rice a coffee-cupful of tomato ketchup and giving the whole a dusting of grated Parmesan.

APPENDIX.

HINTS ON BAKING AT HOME.

FANCY bread has become an almost essential portion
of the English breakfast. It is susceptible of con-
siderable variety, and in view of this fact I have
suggested various kinds of rolls, scones, bannocks,
&c., in the *menus*. These have now to be explained.
While many of them must, of course, be old familiar
friends, some, I think, will be found uncommon ; at
any rate, there are twenty different sorts to choose
from, and as I propound the simplest possible system
of baking—with baking powder—little or no difficulty
should be experienced in working out the whole
category. Still, it must be admitted that as in all
branches of cookery, so in this, experience in regard
to details is necessary. Flours vary in quality.
With some less moistening fluid is necessary than
with others, in consequence of which exact proportions may sometimes not be hit off without an
experiment or two. With perseverance, however,
success is certain. A very important factor in the
operation is the oven. This demands close obser-
vance on the part of the cook, for ovens seem to

be as variable in their dispositions as human beings. A great advance has, however, been made in the construction of ranges, and happy is the home baker who possesses one with regulating power in regard to the heating of the baking apparatus. In some (I might say *all*) ordinary old-fashioned kitchen stoves the ovens are deficient in bottom heat, quite an essential feature in the baking of bread, cakes, *soufflés*, &c., and many a cook is, I fear, unfairly blamed for failures that might be traced to this defect in her appliances.

If fancy bread baking be carried out nearly every day, it is desirable that the cook should keep a set of utensils separately for this branch of her work—a shallow white enamelled milk pan, two wooden spoons of a largish size, a dozen round patty pans for ordinary rolls two and a half inches in diameter, half a dozen muffin rings, a wire drainer as used by confectioners, a baking sheet, and six special tins for French rolls.

The milk pan is recommended for the kneading of the dough, for which process the wooden spoons should be used. Thus, work with the hands is unnecessary, and greater lightness is obtained. If little round rolls be set in buttered patty pans they preserve their shape and bake nicely, and French roll tins are useful in a similar manner.

Touching materials, I recommend Yeatman's baking powder, because I have had sixteen years' experience of it, and have proved its reliability. In regard to flours, there are many varieties to choose from. For white fancy bread such as rolls, Hungarian or Vienna is considered the best, while for the different digestive cakes, scones, &c., brown flour, wholemeal or wheatmeal, oatmeal, barley-meal, Indian-meal and so on, are called into play. It is, I presume, scarcely necessary to add that all flour used in baking should be as dry as possible.

In the directions given for home baking on a small scale, it often happens that certain rule-of-thumb dry measures are given which cannot be considered definite, such as "cups" of flour, and "teaspoonfuls" — "heaped up" or not, as the case may be — of baking powder. Many find it difficult to decide what cup to choose, and all teaspoons are not made exactly the same size. I have accordingly adopted a system of weights for everything, excepting a salt-spoonful of salt, which have been carefully verified and can be trusted.

Touching "a saltspoonful of salt." It will be found on careful examination that a heaped up ordinary kitchen saltspoonful weighs two drachms, and a mere bowlful *not* heaped up half that quantity. For the sake of clearness, then, I would explain that when I say "a saltspoonful" I mean the former, and when I say "a small saltspoonful" I mean the latter.

With liquids there is less risk of ambiguity than with dry measure, for you cannot "heap" them up —a full tablespoonful may be accepted as a fixed quantity, *i.e.*, four tablespoonfuls equal half a gill or a common *sherry* glass, for the term *wine*glass is not explicit.

1. HOT ROLLS.—For eight rolls one and a half ounce each, take eight ounces of flour, a quarter of an ounce of Yeatman's powder, a saltspoonful of salt, and half an ounce of butter. Spread the flour in the enamelled pan, sprinkle the baking powder and salt over its surface, mix well, then rub the butter into it. This having been done, begin to moisten with milk

or buttermilk by degrees, working the dough with the wooden spoons. Nine tablespoonfuls, provided that the flour be of fine quality, should suffice if the operator work skilfully. When ready, turn this out upon a floured pastry board, divide the dough into eight equal portions, pat them into a round shape with the spoons, and place them in eight buttered patty pans. Arrange these upon a baking sheet, wet the surfaces of the rolls with a brush that has been dipped into milk, and slip the sheet into the oven, which should be rather brisk. When the rolls have risen and taken a pale brown colour, they may be taken out of the oven, turned out of the patty pans, and served in a hot napkin. Time, from twelve to fifteen minutes.

2. FRENCH ROLLS.—For six French rolls exactly double the quantities given in the preceding recipe should be taken, with the addition of one fresh egg. Work in the same way, adding the egg well beaten at the commencement of the moistening, then enough milk to form a firm dough. When smooth, turn this out on a floured pastry board, divide it into six portions, and pat these into elongated oval shapes ; lay these in well-buttered French roll tins, brush them over with milk, and set them upon a baking sheet, finishing as in the previous case.

3. VIENNA ROLLS.—The difference here consists in the shape alone. Having worked the dough as for French rolls, turn it out on a floured board, divide it into six portions, roll these out into sausage shapes an inch and a half thick in the centre, tapering somewhat towards the ends, curve them in the form of crescents, lay them on a buttered baking tin, brush them over with milk, and bake about fifteen minutes.

4. KNOTTED ROLLS.—Here again variety is obtained by shaping the dough in a different manner : a crisp crusty roll is thus produced. Roll the portions of dough out into long tubular shapes the thickness of your little finger, tie them in knots, and finish as in the case of Vienna rolls.

5. INDIAN-MEAL ROLLS.—For these the proportions of flour only are altered, viz., twelve ounces of fine flour to four ounces Indian-meal (maize flour). For the rest the ingredients are the same as for French rolls, and the method of work also. They may be shaped as " Hot Rolls " (No. 1), and baked in patty pans.

6. BROWN ROLLS.—In this case substitute the best wholemeal, well dried, for flour ; in other respects proceed as detailed for " Hot Rolls " (No. 1). Another wholesome variation can be obtained by a mixture in these proportions : Five ounces of wholemeal to three of fine well-dried oatmeal, while a milder digestive roll is got by substituting flour for wholemeal, and mixing three ounces of fine oatmeal with it.

7. SIR HENRY THOMPSON'S WHOLEMEAL CAKES. —" Take two pounds of coarsely-ground whole wheat-meal, and add half a pound of fine flour, or, better still, the same weight of *fine* Scotch oatmeal. Mix thoroughly with a sufficient quantity of baking powder and a little salt ; then rub in two ounces of butter and make into dough—using a wooden spoon—with cold skimmed milk or milk and water, soft in consistence, so that it can almost be poured into the tin ring, which gives it form when baked. In this manner it is to be quickly made into flat cakes (like tea cakes), and baked on a tin, the rings used being about an inch high and seven or eight inches in diameter, each

enclosing a cake. Put them without delay into a quick oven at the outset, letting them be finished thoroughly, at a lower temperature."

"The object of making this bread in flat cakes or in scones is to ensure a light and well-cooked product. It is difficult to ensure these two qualities in the form of loaves except of the smallest size. A larger proportion of oatmeal, if preferred, can be adopted by either method."

N.B.—Half an ounce of Yeatman's baking powder and a saltspoonful of salt per pound of meal will be found correct.

8. MUFFINS.—Sift together a pound of fine flour, an ounce of Yeatman's powder, and two saltspoonfuls of salt, stir in enough milk by degrees to form a smooth, but rather stiff, batter. Butter four muffin rings, lay them on a buttered baking sheet well heated, half fill them with the batter, and put them in the oven. When the batter has risen level with the top of the rings, turn them gently and bake till a good straw colour, when take out the tin, turn the muffins out of the rings, open them, toast slightly on the inside, butter them, fold the two pieces together again, and serve at once. About a pint of milk or a little more will be probably required to form the batter. Time, about twenty-five minutes.

9. CRUMB MUFFINS.—Weigh half a pound of stale white breadcrumb, eight ounces of flour, and half an ounce of baking powder. Beat up two eggs. Soak the crumbs till soft in warm milk. Mix the flour and baking powder well, adding a saltspoonful of salt. Combine the two, diluting first with the beaten eggs, and then with enough milk, if necessary, to form a stiff batter. Put this into buttered muffin rings upon

a hot buttered baking tin, and bake in a quick oven fifteen minutes.

10. SALLY LUNNS, NOT SWEETENED.—Rub two ounces of butter into a pound of flour, with which half an ounce of baking powder has been thoroughly sifted and a saltspoonful of salt. Convert this into dough by first mixing with it two well-beaten eggs, and then milk enough by degrees to bring it to the consistency of thick batter. For the rest, treat this as explained for " Crumb Muffins."

11. TEA CAKES, UNSWEETENED.—Beat up a couple of eggs in a bowl, warm a quarter of a pint of milk, and melt in it two ounces of butter. Mix these together well, and then stir in by degrees three-quarters of a pound of flour, with which half an ounce of baking powder and a saltspoonful of salt have been well incorporated. If necessary, add a little more milk or flour, as the case may be, to obtain the consistency of a firm batter. Put into rings, and proceed as in No. 8.

12. SCONES.—Under this denomination there are several varieties. The ordinary English sort may be described in the following manner: With one pound of flour mix well a saltspoonful of salt and half an ounce of Yeatman's powder; then rub into this two ounces of butter, and when that has been thoroughly done, commence moistening with a well-beaten egg and enough milk (something rather less than half a pint) to form a light dough. Lay this on a floured board, roll it out half an inch thick, divide this into a dozen neat oblongs. Bake on a buttered baking tin in a hot oven eight or ten minutes, and when nicely browned, serve piled up in a hot napkin.

13. BARLEY-MEAL SCONES.—Follow the previous

recipe, substituting barley-meal for flour. Properly speaking, according to old Scottish custom, these scones should be cooked on a "girdle," *i.e.*, a thick circular piece of iron about a foot and a half in diameter, which should be suspended or held over a clear fire and heated till a few grains of salt laid upon its surface crackle ; this having been brushed off, the cakes or scones should be laid upon the girdle, occasionally turned, and taken off with a slice (the "spurtle") when they are nicely browned. But this process is in these days of closed ranges unnecessary, ingenious as it may have been when the cook had to do her best with only a primitive open fire to work with. Scones can now be cooked "girdle"-wise in a thick iron plate or frying-pan on the hot plate of the range, or on a baking sheet in the oven. A good bottom heat is obviously the thing that is needed. You can see scones beautifully cooked by electricity at Messrs. Verity's, in Regent Street, on this principle. But to return to the case in hand. Having mixed the dough as in No. 11, turn it out upon a board, dredge it over with flour, and roll it out a third of an inch thick, cut this into three-inch squares, double the opposite corners over, forming three-cornered shapes, and bake on a buttered tin in the oven eight or ten minutes ; or lay them upon a heated iron frying-pan upon the hot plate, and treat them in the manner just described for the girdle scones.

14. BROWN FLOUR SCONES.—Mix with a pound of wheatmeal half an ounce of baking powder and a saltspoonful of salt ; rub two ounces of butter into this, and when that has been done, commence moistening with a well-beaten fresh egg, adding just enough milk or buttermilk to bring it to the consis-

tence of a light dough. Finish as described for No. 11.

15. BANNOCKS.—A pound of fine oatmeal, a salt-spoonful of salt, and half an ounce of baking powder having been sifted and mixed, rub into it an ounce of butter, and then moisten with water in sufficient quantity to make a thick dough. Roll this out as thin as possible, divide it into quarters, and halve each of them; lay these one by one on a heated iron frying-pan upon the hot plate, bake, turning them on each side. Toast afterwards in front of the fire till crisp.

16. IRISH BANNOCKS.—Warm half a pint of milk and dissolve in it three ounces of butter; mix into this a pound of wheatmeal, half an ounce of baking powder, and a saltspoonful of salt. Mix to a stiff dough. Turn this upon the board, roll it out three-quarters of an inch thick, and cut into six cakes. Bake in the manner just described, and serve dusted over with flour on a hot napkin.

17. OAT CAKES.—As a rule, the directions given for these wholesome cakes counsel the cook to roll them out as thin as possible. This, of course, is simply a matter of taste, and with cheese perhaps the thin cake is very nice, but for breakfast I think a thicker cake is better. For these take one pound of oatmeal—coarse or fine, as may be preferred—rub into this two ounces of butter with a small teaspoonful of salt, and then moisten with sufficient water to make a smooth dough. Pat this into a round mass and lay it upon a floured board, roll it out not less than *a quarter of an inch* thick, cut this into three and a half inch squares, halve these by cutting them across from corner to corner, forming triangular shapes, and

bake in the pan till firm and thoroughly done. Dust over with sifted meal and serve in a hot napkin.

18. DEVILLED BISCUIT. — Take a dozen plain water biscuits, or six " Bath Olivers." If the former be only two inches in diameter, six can be done at a time in a large, or three in a medium, pan as follows : Put an ounce of butter into a large, or half an ounce into a small, frying-pan over a low fire : as soon as it begins to melt, lay the biscuits upon it, turning them over the fire till the butter browns, pepper well with grill seasoning (page 37). Put them on a very hot dish, and pour the browned butter over them, and serve. Or if liked very dry, lay them, after having been thus cooked, on a wire drainer, and set them in the oven for a minute or two, serving *as hot as possible*, closely covered in a hot silver dish.

Biscuit à l'Indienne is prepared as the foregoing, but curry powder is dusted over it instead of the plain seasoning of pepper and salt. Some even like an addition of a couple of drops of tabasco on each biscuit.

Bath Olivers or three-inch water biscuits ought to be done separately one after another.

19. CRUMPETS.—In London and most towns crumpets can be so easily procured from " the manufacturer," that very few people take the trouble to make them at home. In the country this is different ; besides, there may be some who, among other experiments, would like to try this:—Thoroughly mix together twelve ounces of Vienna flour, a small saltspoonful of salt, and three-quarters of an ounce of Yeatman's baking powder ; then stir in an ounce of butter, melted, one egg well beaten, and enough milk to form a smooth batter. With this half fill six or

eight well-buttered muffin rings, which should be laid beforehand on a heated iron pan. Watch, and when the batter rises somewhat, turn each crumpet carefully, and finish the baking without further turning. Toast lightly, butter, and serve in the usual manner, Coming straight from the pan in this way, they will be found nicer than those bought cold and toasted afterwards.

20. SOUTHERN INDIAN CRUMPETS, OR "APUMS." —Put one pound and a half of rice flour into a pan, dilute it to a stiff paste with lukewarm water, in which half an ounce of fresh German yeast has been dissolved. Let this remain all night; next day moisten this with the juice of a cocoanut to the consistency of firmish batter, and put a gill of this at a time into a heated and buttered pan over the hot plate, covering the pan closely. When nicely risen and browned round the edges the "apum" is ready. Repeat the process with similar quantities of the mixture till all of it is expended : serve very hot on a napkin, dusted over with salt.

Cocoanut juice is made as follows : Scrape the nutty part of a cocoanut into fine shreds, put these in a bowl, pour scalding water over them, moistening them well. After half an hour's infusion, strain the liquid into a bowl, and putting the nut scrapings into a piece of muslin, squeeze all the moisture out of them into the strained juice. This extract of cocoanut is what the Southern Indian cook uses in curry making under the name of " cocoanut milk," a fluid that it resembles in appearance. The water inside the nut is not " cocoanut milk " from this standpoint.

21. OATMEAL PORRIDGE.—This is a deservedly popular thing for breakfast. To prepare it, weigh a

couple of ounces of oatmeal, put three-quarters of a pint of water in a saucepan, set it on the fire and bring it to the boil; cast into it a *pinch* (the eighth of an ounce) of salt, and then dredge in the oatmeal, stirring with a wooden spoon while the operation is being carried out. Simmer for forty minutes, by which time the oatmeal should have absorbed the water and be swollen and soft. It can now be served accompanied by a jug of hot milk, sugar or salt being added according to taste, the latter obviously for choice. Cream is, of course, a favourite adjunct with many, but does it not detract from the well-known wholesomeness of the porridge? I think so.

Those who like their porridge at its best will find the following process a good one:—Let the prepared oatmeal be sent in in its saucepan, set this on a spirit lamp in the breakfast-room, stirring in cold milk in sufficient quantity to bring the porridge to the desired consistency; wait till air bubbles begin to rise to the surface, and turn it into a very hot soup plate. *Hot* milk can be used if liked, but remember that there is a difference in the flavour of boiled and unboiled milk. By this plan a properly hot porridge is certain in a couple of minutes.

The proportions given will yield two large or three small portions. If the oatmeal absorbs the water too quickly in the cooking, additional hot water should be stirred in. Some oatmeals are more floury than others, and as much as a pint of water may be needed for two ounces.

22. DRY TOAST.—A very simple thing to be sure, yet how often is it maltreated—scorched outside, spongy within, and flabby? The bread should not be new; it should be cut in quarter inch slices, and

toasted at *some little distance* from the clear smokeless
embers, patiently, till each side has turned a nice pale
golden brown. Sir Henry Thompson's dry toast is
made in this way :—The slices are cut somewhat
thicker — three-eighths of an inch — and slightly
coloured on both sides. A sharp knife is then passed
horizontally through the softish centre part, making
two pieces of each slice. The inner sides are now
toasted, and nice crisp dry toast is the result.

23. ANTI-FAT TOAST, for those who have to think
twice about eating bread, is easily made as follows :—
Cut a stale tin-baked loaf into thin slices (one-eighth
of an inch thick at the outside), lay these on a wire
drainer in the oven till they crispen and turn yellowish
brown. If a good quantity of it be prepared, this
toast can be kept in a biscuit tin, and will be quite
nice for two or three days. Excellent whether for
breakfast, luncheon, or dinner.

INDEX.

—◆—

DISHES OF FISH.

DISHES OF MEAT.

DISHES OF EGGS.

FANCY BREAD, ROLLS, &c.

MISCELLANEOUS.

UNWIN BROTHERS, LIMITED, PRINTERS, WOKING AND LONDON.